SAVE YOUR

HOME

without losing your mind or your money

BY #1 BEST SELLING AUTHOR

ANNA CUEVAS

BEST KNOWN AS THE LOAN MODIFICATION GURU

volition
PRESS

SAVE YOUR HOME

without losing your mind or your money

ANNA CUEVAS

www.TheLoanModGuru.com

ISBN 978-0-9837556-3-0

Library of Congress Control Number:
2011932556

Copyright© 2011

Volition Press

volition
PRESS

Printed in the United States of America

IN GRATITUDE:

Mom – For being the greatest role model of strength and work ethic.

Jane Komarov – My GI Jane! There are absolutely no words that can describe what you have meant to me and this project. Without you, I would never have gotten this far. I am eternally grateful for you. Thank You!!

Oscar Cuevas – For holding down the fort so I can get this project done, and for bragging about me.

Christina Cuevas – For taking over my role, and getting things done so I can get my creative force out to the world.

Jason Cuevas – For always supporting me through this entire process and giving me great insight and perspective.

Jake Cuevas – For always listening to my ideas and helping me make them better and make them happen.

Berny Dohrmann and CEO Space – Thank you for your remarkable spirit and incredible vision, you inspire me to live my purpose on a daily basis, and you remind me of the WHY.

Michael Masterson, Early to Rise – For showing me the power of the Internet.

Mike Koenigs and Rocket Helstrom at Traffic Geyser - For reminding me that it is my responsibility to bring this information to the millions of homeowners waiting desperately to hear it. Your commitment to excellence is contagious.

Greg Reid – For being so approachable and willing to help steer me in the right direction to get this information out to people, thank you for being you, you are truly inspiring and "always good."

David Corbin – For being the best mentor anyone could ever hope for. You are just THE best ever, and I am so grateful to you for your incredible influence in shaping my thinking to an extraordinary level.

Michelle Price – For giving me some fantastic ideas on how to expand my message to homeowners in need.

Les Brown – For letting me be a part of the "Fight for Your Dreams" project and being such an inspiration to so many.

Patti McKenna – For being an amazing book diva, you are remarkable, thank you for helping me get this book over the mountain.

Karen Barranco – For taking the initiative to design the amazing cover. I am grateful and in awe of your talent.

Cathy Fosco – For your hard work in working on ways to spread this message of hope. You are one amazing lady.

Jeremy Gutsche – Trend Hunter for giving me rule #1 "Relentlessly obsess about my story."

TABLE OF CONTENTS

DISCLAIMER

The information contained in this book is purely for educational purposes. Nothing in this book can or should be construed as giving legal advice or practicing law. We are not attorneys. You are advised to consult competent legal counsel. Your reliance on the information presented within this book is at your own risk.

The authors make no warrantees, assurances or claims to the legitimacy, accuracy, or completeness of the information contained within this work, explicit or implied. This is information that we want to present to you for your consideration. It is the result of thousands of hours of research, actual cases, personal experience and interviews with industry experts. We believe the information is accurate to the best of our knowledge.

Do your own research and discover your own truth.

This book is meant as a guide to fight for your home through the loan modification process. At the time of publication, the programs available vary from the government's HAMP program to different types of in-house modifications. Regardless of the program, the key lies in remaining positive, being organized, being informed and fighting for your home. You can use the tools in this book to fight through all of the different processes.

The programs come and go, but the principles of the loan modification process and how to fight back remain steady, if you know what to look for.

They said you could do this by yourself...without any help...Well, you can do it yourself, but you do need guidance!

REAL SAVE YOUR HOME SUCCESS STORIES

What Others are Saying About Anna Cuevas, The Loan Modification Guru!

Anna Cuevas is one of the most influential experts in the Home Mortgage business. She is not only a loan expert who is at the top of her field, but a phenomenal person with exceptional knowledge and compassion for others. She is led by her spiritual beliefs, which enable her to share and give to others like no one I have ever encountered...she provided me with information I needed to save my home that I couldn't find anywhere else. Anna inspired me to have strength, hope, and faith, which transformed my life. I highly recommend her book, Save Your Home; she will not only provide you with the knowledge to save your home, she will touch your soul, as she did mine, with her inspiration. Thank You, Anna, from the bottom of my heart.

- Allison C.
Washington State

Testimonial from "Mario and Betty, "A Featured Success Story in *Save Your Home*:

I had already given up all hope and was at the end of my own ability to try and save my home. I had been let down by 6 modification companies, 3 of which were law firms, and not one of them was there for me and my family when we desperately needed their help.

Here I was, a real estate and finance professional for almost 29 years, and I found myself in a position that I could have never imagined myself to be in. No, this could never happen to people like us. I had only heard of those individuals who suffered the loss of their long-lived dream and comforts of their homes through others and by watching the housing crisis thicken. It seemed that all of these people who were losing their homes to foreclosure were just like us, the same hardworking individuals, real people that had an unfortunate occurrence in their lives, and in the end, they lost their American dream. How devastatingly impacted we were, and we didn't have an ounce of faith or trust left in anyone at that time who professed to be "The Hope for Home Owners" or "The Modification Specialists."

That never existed in our year-long search for relief and never was made a reality in our life. That changed one evening, up again at 3 a.m., unable to sleep from the depression and thoughts that continually saturated my mind that we were going to lose our dream and everything that we had worked so hard for and for so long. "The

Loan Mod Guru" was the heading on a website. What did I have to lose? I read the content and testimonials from people who had success with this so called "Loan Mod Guru." It touched my heart and gave me a sense of peace, because these people were so overwhelmed with joy and spoke so fondly of her and of the miracles that she had performed by saving their homes. Only four months after our initial conversation and meeting, we had our Trial Loan Modification. We had endlessly fought for our home for one year, and never received help, hope, or faith from anyone, and in one day, her words remedied all of our doubts and feelings of loss.

If there are such things as "angels" sent from heaven, and I do believe there are, I know that one of those angels is named Anna Cuevas. Thank you, my friend, for saving our American Dream.

I highly recommend her book, Save your Home. I know it will truly help you during one of the most trying times in your life and will give you the same peace I have today.

Thank you so much, Anna, for showing us that there is truth that stands the test of time.

- Mario and Betty
Riverside, CA

After trying for almost a year to get help from our mortgage company and complying with every single item that they requested, after being lied to, misled, discouraged, and denied multiple times, being told by multiple "Persons in Authority" that we had no option other than to let them have our home, and receiving a notice of trustee sale on our home on December 4, 2010, notifying us of the sale of our home set for Christmas Eve, December 24, 2010, we had just about given up all hope of saving our home.

Not knowing what to do or where to go, my wife learned about a person who was claiming to be able to help people like ourselves and empower them to be able to save their homes. That person is Anna Cuevas. As God is my witness, it IS true. We have experienced it. Not only is our home saved from foreclosure, but also our payment was reduced by 46%.

If you are struggling with your loan modification, Save Your Home is a MUST READ!

- Jim
Perris, CA

FOREWORD

GREG S. REID

As a motivational speaker and author, I can often be heard telling clients and audiences to "keep smilin'." Especially during trying times, people tend to dwell on their problems, instead of focusing on their opportunities. Sometimes, we allow negativity and pessimism a chance to overtake our success, causing us to stop whatever it is we're undertaking...at the exact moment when we are closest to achieving it. In my book, *Three Feet from Gold*, I discuss this tendency... most people drop the shovel and give up when they're only three feet from reaping the rewards of their work. That's unfortunate, because I believe if they only knew how close they were, they wouldn't have given up—they would have dug even faster.

Anna Cuevas understands this concept. She's helped thousands realize how important it is to put forth extra effort when it appears their situation is becoming increasingly bleak. Many homeowners who have followed her proven strategies and system of loan modification have benefitted from the perseverance it took to dig a little deeper to find an acceptable solution to their circumstances. Together with adopting the positive attitude that Anna encourages, it's these homeowners who exemplify the Three Feet from Gold principle—frankly, quitters can't win. If you truly want success, you have to keep on keepin' on and keep smilin'.

Difficult times are trying, but they do present opportunities. Anna Cuevas has done her homework—she understands the mortgage process, and she knows the opportunities available to at-risk homeowners. She also knows that it's when homeowners believe there is no hope that the real hope is at arm's length. Follow the strategies she provides in this book and you just might find that your opportunities are worth continuing to fight for. Perseverance brings rewards.

The formula for success in saving a business, a relationship, or a home is an easy one: $P + T + A2 + F =$ Success.

$$Passion + Talent + Action\ and\ Association + Faith = Success$$

If you combine your passion with your talent, then take action to make it happen and surround yourself with people who can help you, and carry it out with a strong dose of faith, you'll produce success. In this book, you'll learn gain the knowledge to have the talent, the steps, the people, and the faith to make your passion a possibility.

Anna's passion is helping others navigate the process of saving their home. She works tirelessly to provide them with the advice and assistance they dearly need. As a loan modification guru with years of experience, she has the talent and knowledge to know what works and how to get it done to achieve positive results. Then, she takes homeowners through the steps one by one, telling them how to take the appropriate action and who to direct it to. She's the trusted association you need and can count on. Added to her Passion, Talent, Action, and Association is a strong dose of Faith, something that's not only refreshing, but necessary, as you make the commitment to save your home. With each of the components in place, Anna Cuevas and her book, *Save Your Home,* are your formula for success.

Anna truly believes in helping the many people who are in danger of losing their home. She doesn't do this to get rich quick or to become famous. She's simply the kind of person that wants to share her expertise to benefit others. Often, all that she asks for in return is that the recipient passes it on. Pass on your newfound knowledge and optimism. Let others know that there is hope, if they keep on digging. You're closer to success than you know—now that you have this book in your hands, you're just three feet from gold and even closer to saving your home!

Keep smilin'!

Greg S. Reid

AUTHOR'S PREFACE

The vast number of foreclosures has reached epic proportions and is affecting people in every economic class. States, counties, cities, and neighborhoods are affected in ways that most people cannot fathom. In July of 2010, the Associated Press reported that 1.7 million homeowners have received a foreclosure-related notice. I repeat: 1.7 million! Of these 1.7 million homeowners that are late on their mortgage, approximately 1 million of them stand to lose their homes this year alone. Let's change that!

Everyone is overwhelmed; the homeowners are frozen with anxiety. The lenders cannot keep up with the workload, and everyone, I mean everyone, is frustrated about the process. People need help; what they don't know is that they need to empower themselves and take control of their situation with real information, organization, and determination. This is the only way you can get real help as the crooks have come out of the woodwork, and people do not know whom to trust. The very system that is broken is preaching to people to do this by themselves, but everyone going through this feels lost and strangled in the red tape. People are very scared.

This book was written so those people can know that someone does care about them and wants them to be empowered. With this information, they don't have to be afraid and can operate with confidence, instead of fear, and they can resume their life and once again take a deep breath and finally get a good night's sleep. This is what this information—if followed step-by-step—can do for you.

Many times when customers call their lenders, they receive what amounts to different kinds of inaccurate guesses that serve as answers to life-changing questions. I am not here to bad mouth anyone, because we all deserve respect. They are not doing this to be mean or because they actually want you to lose your home; they really are doing their jobs the best they can with the information they have available. Frankly, I think this kind of customer interaction information rarely makes it to the top executives until the squeaky wheels bring it to light. BE the squeaky wheel if you have to, but be an informed squeaky wheel.

While many people working for mortgage lenders are just doing their 9-to-5 jobs, there are some jewels that are willing to go above and beyond. For most, though, it is just a job, like in every other industry. On top of that, you can imagine the stress from dealing with all of the distraught borrowers who are sometimes not very nice to them. They want to run, not walk, as fast as they can out of the building when quitting time rolls around. We need to be aware at all times that most people in this country have been trained in the industrial revolution/factory worker mentality and will do just that without empathy or outside-of-the-box thinking.

I honestly don't think that the average person working for a lender goes home after hours and scours through hours of fun reading on the government's HAMP guidelines, even though this is what it would take to know the rules. If you stop and think about it, would you? In this case, it is up to you if you want to save your house. Unfortunately, there isn't enough time in their work day to learn the ins and outs of all of the programs, as they have files to work on and are buried knee deep in their caseloads. You can make a difference to them by being as nice as you can to everyone with whom you come into contact.

No matter what, don't let anyone shake your inner peace, confidence, and determination. I hope you make a choice to make a difference in other people's lives. You might just help the next person. It's true that a positive attitude creates a ripple; it is contagious, and it helps life's affairs run more smoothly and awakens people's desire to help you. A positive attitude, coupled with taking the necessary action, will affect your outcome in any situation, including the one you are currently facing. Even if you feel frustrated, be the person who is calm, cool, and collected at all times. Regardless of what they say to you, you will get a lot further this way; you may make a difference in their day, and you'll feel a million times better in the process. Heck, you might even make a friend.

It is the responsibility of you, the homeowner, to empower yourself with information so that you know exactly what you need to do. Don't expect in any situation that what you have been told is always 100% accurate, because in my experience, things are NOT always what they seem. But if you know your stuff, you can fight for your home effectively. Question everything. Now is not the time to assume that you are being given accurate information. THIS IS YOUR HOME we are talking about, and this matters most to you! Yes, you may have to fax the same paper 20 times, but at this point, you have to face the reality of the situation. If you have to fax it 20 times, then that is what you have to do. At the same time, you must become informed, you must follow up, and you must do all of this with a good attitude or it is like drinking poison and expecting someone else to die. You are killing yourself when you let anything affect your inner peace, regardless how bad it is. Decide to fight.

We have the means to change our reactions. A very large percentage of the time, the most horrible chain of events we dream up and worry about doesn't happen. If we only direct our thoughts and energy into those negative outcomes, they will surely arrive. It is time to slap some water on our faces, and take a walk in nature everyday to regain our inner peace. We must direct more energy into learning what our rights are and what the rules of this game are. It is time to focus on the positive outcome we want—focus on saving your home and doing the work to make it happen by becoming your own best advocate. This is what it takes, and as long as you know this from the start, you can take it on.

Many people have lost their homes because they received a letter stating that they were denied modification, but they failed to verify the information for accuracy. I know many of those people lost their homes needlessly. Many people are told erroneous information over the phone, so they pack up and move and lose their home, but the information they were given was wrong. This saddens me deeply. Unless you empower yourself with knowledge, these things can continue to happen in all areas of your life. It is time to remember who you are and take charge and not allow things to happen to you without investigation and verification. I know it doesn't sound easy, but if you change your attitude, you can move mountains.

The effects of foreclosure on family dynamics can be momentous. It causes stress-related illnesses, lowers productivity for employers, causes divorces, and can advance the progression of alcoholism. For children in the home, it leads to bad grades due to a tremendous amount of fear, anxiety, and panic. There are overwhelming thoughts of helplessness that come with the very real possibility of losing your home. Coupled with the silent shame associated with the stigma that foreclosure brings, this wreaks havoc on so many different levels. Yet, some people still believe that the people who purchased homes beyond their means are the only ones who deserve to be in this position. This is so very far from the truth. There are many reasons and factors that cause foreclosure. The very person that believes this can lose their job tomorrow and end up a victim of the foreclosure crisis.

With unemployment levels at a concerning high and the job market so dismal, many people have to accept jobs which pay 1/4 or even 1/2 of what they used to make. In addition, many cannot find a job for time frames of a full year or two; they are also struggling with the thought of losing their home and being both unemployed, as well as homeless. For too many, this is a reality, not just a bad dream. I am a believer that when bad things happen, it lowers the quality of your thoughts and, therefore, permits many bad things to continue to happen. Change the channel of your thoughts, and you will begin to see positive changes. I think you can do this! Expect ONLY Miracles and Question Authority!

I will leave you with these quotes:

"I advise you to say your dream is possible and then overcome all inconveniences, ignore all the hassles and take a running leap through the hoop, even if it is in flames."
- Les Brown

"Whether you think you can or you think you can't, either way, you are right."
- Henry Ford

Anna Cuevas
San Diego, California
May, 2011

DEDICATION

Thank you to God through Christ and the Holy Spirit, who spared my life from ovarian cancer with a miracle. Thank you for entrusting me to carry this message of hope forward to homeowners that are suffering and using me as your instrument to serve others. You are the way, the truth, and the light!

To my amazing family:

My mom, Maria Jimenez, who brought me into this world, showed me about caring for others, empathy, and taking a stand and escalating what you believe in. You are such a special lady!

My husband and soul mate, Oscar Cuevas, who has always believed in me and works hard for our family. You are the one true love of my life!

My oldest daughter, Christina, my biggest fan - thank you for always striving to be the best. Your take-charge mentality made this book possible. I am so proud of you. Since you were born, you have always inspired me to do great things!

My son, Josh, thank you for your support of me and welcoming me into your life, always listening to my ideas and thoughts. You have greatness within. Your kind and happy spirit is contagious!

My daughter, Jen, you have such a great heart, thank you for always listening to my ideas and thoughts with such enthusiasm and interest; you have helped me in so many ways. You amaze me!

My son, Jason, thank you for being such an amazing guy, always bringing me joy and laughter, and believing in this cause and in me with such conviction and confidence. You are so great!

My son, Jake, your wisdom, maturity, and soul are something to behold and beyond comprehension. Thank you for being my confidant. You are so awesome!

My muse, Jack, the famous Jack Russell. Thanks for bringing me childlike fun in the middle of a chaotic life; guarding me and sitting right by my side for the entire writing of this book. You even stopped me when I went overboard by blocking the keyboard. You are the best dog ever!

Last, but certainly not least, this book is dedicated to my loyal homeowners. You have touched my heart and inspired me to pay my blessings forward. You humble me with your **STRENGTH TO FIGHT ON!**

INTRODUCTION

A t this time of uncertainty, there is one thing that is still in your power: Knowledge. How can they expect you to do this by yourself and do it right if you are not given the information and tools to be successful, or if you're not given the information to keep pushing on even in the event of a denial from your lender?

Everywhere you turn, all you hear is that you can modify your own loan and you can work with your lender directly; you are hearing it from your lender, from the government, and from the media. The problem is no one is telling you what to expect or what you need to know to be able to get this done on your own, with the confidence you need, to work through the process.

There are all sorts of advertisements and knocks on the door from people you may want to trust, but they may not always have your best interest at heart. Or, they may not really be in a position to help you the way they say they can. Many are taking advantage of people in this vulnerable situation. Don't let that be you. Arm yourself with as much information and knowledge as possible. Let a short sale only be an option if you are sure that trying to modify your loan is not a better solution.

You can do this yourself but ONLY if you are armed with the right tools and information. I have witnessed the information I am giving you in this book; used directly in the trenches, saving the homes of countless families. Pay close attention, stay focused, determined, and believe you can do it.

It is my responsibility to share the knowledge I have on this matter with you. This is why I decided to write this book.

Affirmations

I have included affirmations throughout this book to ingrain thoughts of success into your mind, as I have a belief that this is a key ingredient to actually succeeding.

This is why:

Words have power – This is worth considering for a moment.

There is no doubt that you are feeling frustrated, and I am a believer of giving yourself a break; stop, drop, and roll (just kidding).

Stop, take a deep breath, and speak affirmations for success in this situation. Do this instead of the usual tendency to allow ourselves to throw a tantrum, be victimized, gripe, moan, cuss, and give up. (Hopefully, you don't flail on the ground anymore—just kidding again!)

It may take more than a few words to shift the thoughts we have toward freaking out over our frustrations, especially with regard to dealing with something so close to our heart, like our home. However, we cannot deny that words carry a lot of power, so positive-power words can help you come from a place of confidence and success.

Anna Cuevas

SECTION ONE

CORE ISSUES: GETTING STARTED

CHAPTER ONE

KNOWLEDGE AND ATTITUDE ARE EVERYTHING: QUESTION AUTHORITY

"It is the first responsibility of every citizen to question authority."
— Benjamin Franklin

The Fear of Losing Your Home

D efaulting on your mortgage and facing foreclosure is a very nerve-racking experience. Just keep in mind that the more stressed out and anxious you are about your situation, the less you can accomplish. There are millions of people currently facing foreclosure. You are not alone. You can stand out from the crowd of millions of people who just give up, walk away, and lose their home without ever even trying to save it, if you get the knowledge you need to help you work through this situation. Help is available. You just have to become informed, take action and be ready to work through any frustrations—let it go and keep on trying to get resolution to your mortgage problem. The more knowledge and information you have, and the more you know about the process and how it works, the greater the chances of being successful.

More than 50% of all delinquent borrowers never contact or speak with their lender. Many are not even aware that there may be help available. I believe this is mainly because of fear. Fear paralyzes people. The fear of the unknown holds us back from many things in life. You don't have to let fear take control of you. It doesn't have to be that way. Get informed, get prepared, and take action. There are programs and solutions for you!

You just have to take the first step, and the first step is for you to take control of the situation by getting yourself prepared to stand up for yourself. This can only be accomplished with **KNOWLEDGE and INFORMATION.** If you are prepared to take this on yourself, you can accomplish the same results as anyone else, but you have to be ready to fully accept the challenge and work hard on your own behalf.

You have to be ready to treat this as a business transaction. You must be willing to let go of your fear and emotions while working with the lender as these things ONLY get in the way. Try not to get frustrated; it is what it is, and being frustrated is just another hurdle you MUST overcome or it will eat you up. You will get stuck in that feeling which accomplishes nothing, and in the end, may cost you not only your home, but your sanity, as well – **DON'T LET THAT HAPPEN TO YOU,** regardless of anything that happens, your health and sanity are more important than anything material can ever be. Please don't forget that. Think positive and try not to stress. I know it is hard, but do your best to get some fresh air, do some breathing exercises and spend some quality time with your family during this time. You need to be healthy and clear-headed throughout the process. Even when the collection calls come in, feel confident you can only do what you can do—again, do not stress, do not let it get to you. You are the only one who can allow that to affect you. Choose not to let it get to you.

Remember, these people are just doing their job of trying to collect a debt—it says it right on the statement they make to you. Regardless, be polite; tell them you are working on a loan modification. Be honest and don't let the stress of the calls take over your life.

Also, keep in mind that the collection calls still come while you are processing your modification, sometimes even when you have signed one because many times the departments have not communicated with each other. **DON'T TAKE IT PERSONALLY!!**

IN ORDER FOR THIS PROCESS TO BE SUCCESSFUL, YOU MUST CONSTANTLY REMIND YOURSELF THAT YOU NEED TO STAY IN THE RIGHT STATE OF MIND.

PLEASE REFER TO THE REFERENCE SECTION FOR A GLOSSARY OF TERMS, CONTACTS, EXAMPLES, SAMPLE LETTERS, AND OTHER HELPFUL INFO.

You may ask yourself, "Is it possible to save my home through a loan modification?" Yes, it may not be too late to stop foreclosure. A loan modification may save your home.

When you complete a loan modification, your loan modification company or specialist will renegotiate at least one term change in your loan and get your loan reinstated with a payment you can afford. Its primary result—it usually stops foreclosure.

Affirmation:

I have successfully overcome this current obstacle.

CHAPTER TWO

THE FORECLOSURE PROCESS

E very state has a specific foreclosure process that must be followed. Regardless of what anyone tells you, the law must be followed completely by your lender in order for them to foreclose on your property, and this depends on your particular state law. You should look up the foreclosure law in your state[1] so that you can find out what your timeline is and what your rights are. You also need to be informed as to where in the timeline you currently are and how much time you have to work on saving your home. I have seen a lot of scared people move out the first month they are late on a payment because they fear being evicted by the sheriff. There are foreclosure laws, and then there are eviction laws. **BOTH MUST BE FOLLOWED BEFORE ANYONE CAN EVICT YOU.** *Check with your local superior court for eviction information.*

Where you are in the foreclosure process determines the amount of time you can use as a guide during the processing of your loan modification. Even if you are denied a modification, even more than once, if you are able to change your circumstances, raise your income (i.e., a new job, second job, renting a room, find someone willing to contribute to your household, such

---

[1] Refer to page 133 for information.

as a relative or friend), or reducing your expenses (lowering your insurance, auto, home, property taxes— selling your car, or finding someone who will take over any of your payments), then you can start the process again. Call the lender; tell them that your financials have changed and that you want to resubmit the request for modification. **THEY DON'T KNOW THIS IS WHAT YOU WANT TO DO UNLESS YOU TELL THEM.**

Do not be afraid to ASK questions. Remember: THIS IS YOUR HOME you are trying to save; and frankly, it is more important to you than anyone else, so give it your all.

Remind them over and over that you intend on keeping your home and that you want to work with them to find a program that is an acceptable fit.

Also, if you are denied, don't be afraid to call the lender and ask them why. Get specifics, such as dates and the income and expenses that were used. Compare their numbers to the numbers you already submitted to them.

Keep in mind, humans and computers both make mistakes. Oftentimes, they are using the wrong numbers and this causes you to be denied a modification; it doesn't help if you just accept it and never find out WHY.

Foreclosure: It Can Happen to Anyone?

It was once believed that foreclosure was only for all of those people who bought homes they couldn't afford. No longer is that the case, and I am here to bust that myth. People do not have to hide behind the embarrassment and shame of foreclosure because there are approximately 6 million American homeowners with some sort of a default, ranging from 30-plus days delinquent all the way to a full-blown foreclosure. Homeowners have a lot of company these days when facing this housing crisis, a lot of company, indeed. It is not limited to people of lower income, occupation, and social status. Unemployment is at its highest, countless numbers of people are already off the unemployment insurance grid but are still unemployed, and the census numbers are reporting that one in seven Americans are at poverty level.

You could be the Octomom, or an Orange County housewife reality TV star living in a multi-million dollar mansion, or even the late Ed McMahon of high celebrity status. It could be your sister, your brother, your best friend, or your aging mother. It might be your neighbor, your boss, your employee, or your customers. Heck, it could even be YOU.

Even when it is not currently you, one credit line less for the company you work for and a downsizing could happen and you might be out of a job tomorrow. That is the reality of the situation and the reality of what is happening. I am not one to be negative, but I think it is important to have empathy for our fellow man because foreclosure is devastating to families, neighborhoods, cities, and states. It affects so much more and carries a ripple effect, so many ripples, in fact, that there are too many to mention. What I can mention is that regardless of whether or not you ever have to personally face foreclosure in some roundabout way, it most certainly does affect you. That's why I urge you to do what you can to let your congressman know that the American people need help, real help. They need to cut the red tape associated with the current programs, and they need accountability, especially since we are all footing the bill.

It is important for you to know that many people facing foreclosure today actually were able to afford the homes that they bought at the time they bought them. You should consider this before believing that foreclosure is only for those people that could not afford to buy these homes, or that they deserved those bad loans due to a bad credit profile. Most of them even had reserves in the bank that are now gone, as also is the equity they thought they had, too. Please don't try to take their dignity away, too, while they live in fear of not only being unemployed, but of being homeless, as well.

I urge people facing foreclosure to know their numbers, empower themselves with real knowledge, believe they will prevail, verify everything, follow up, and take action to make what you want happen. To think for yourself, you MUST question authority.

To know your numbers, go to
http://www.theloanmodguru.com today
and BE EMPOWERED!

Fighting Foreclosure with a Rocky Mentality: How to Properly Escalate Your Issues
Don't Guess, Know Your Stuff

When you are experiencing problems in the processing of your file and are not able to get resolution, it is first important for you to have a clear understanding of where you stand before escalating to the next level. It is not a good idea to escalate your file until you are sure you fit within guidelines of the program you are applying for because the last thing you want to do is escalate a file that does not qualify and get rushed through the foreclosure cycle because of it.

Once you are sure that you fit within the guidelines and you have unresolved issues or you cannot get someone to discuss and help you resolve them, then it is time to escalate to the next level. You can do this on the phone, but I prefer doing this in writing to the correspondence address on your mortgage statement.

If you still get nowhere, then keep going up the chain of command by doing research on the company and its key players. New escalation processes have been put in place by government officials and Treasury executives as a result of the Dodd-Frank Act.

In your escalations, include:

A full copy of the file you have submitted along with a detailed, but not too long, cover letter specifying the issues you are experiencing (see letter examples in reference section).

Keep a conversation log, noting every single person you have spoken to, including your servicer, lender, or government officials. Make sure to gather and document this information:

✓ the employee's first and last name,

✓ department,

✓ identification/employee number,

✓ always note the date and time of the call and the number you dialed (*See Conversation Log in Chapter Five*)

✓ Be sure to summarize what was discussed, including any steps you were asked to take, or any missing documentation, fax number, mailing address, or email address (preferred). **Save all fax confirmation sheets and follow up with a letter.**

Call daily and keep these notes for all communications in any form (written, verbal, email, fax, etc.) Save all fax confirmation pages.

I recommend also sending correspondence return receipt requested as much as possible to cover your tracks! Even write letters covering your conversations, such as the one below.

Dear Bank,

On May 21, 2011 at 12:23pm I spoke to Jane Doe and she advised me that the June 1st trustee sale date was put on hold. Please include this confirmation in my file.

Sincerely,

Mr. Homeowner

Being Resourceful and Doing Research to Resolve Issues

This type of escalation is only necessary and suggested after first exhausting all other avenues. Build your case, but if you are in jeopardy of losing your home sooner rather than later, then do not hold back from contacting whomever you have to in order to save your home. But I warn you, know your numbers and be knowledgeable about your entire file first!! Many people fight for files that are impossible to approve for a loan modification; don't let this be you.

Google, Yahoo, Bing, You Tube, and all search engines are your friends. Look through the lender's website for as much information on them. Scour the Internet when searching for:

Executive office addresses, phone and fax numbers to direct your escalation letters:

Vice Presidents, Presidents, and CEO's.

Board Members, if necessary, for blatant escalation.

Government Officials: Congressman, Senator, Governor, FDIC, Treasury, HUD, FHA, Fannie Mae, Freddie Mac.

REMINDER:

Refer to the Resource Section for important contact info and sample letters

Access the Power Within You

"When you get into a tight place and everything goes against you till it seems as though you could not hold on a minute longer, never give up then, for that is just the place and time that the tide will turn."

\- Harriet Beecher Stowe

- It is important for you to access your inner power.

- Visualize the outcome you want and do not deviate from this vision.

- Don't lose <u>yourself</u> in the process of trying not to lose your home.

- Get your mind to the right place with prayer, nature, and meditation.

- Don't allow fear to run your life.

- Take focused and determined action.

- Only allow your best you to show up every day.

- Stay around positive people who believe you can succeed; don't talk to negative ninnies.

- Don't quit even if you are denied.

- For success to happen, you have to have the faith and belief that you will succeed.

- Be grateful for the little things along the way.

- Never stop learning and help others with the good information you gained.

- To be heard you must Be Powerful.

- Be your own best advocate.

- Question authority.

Overcoming Objections

"We have enough people who tell it like it is - now we could use a few who tell it like it can be."

\- Robert Orben

The first thing to remember in overcoming objections is to stay calm. Use all of your charm when speaking to representatives; no one likes to be yelled at or spoken to in a bad tone. Even if you experience rudeness, keep your cool, wish them well, and politely end the call.

Remember this valuable piece of advice: Nothing good EVER comes out of a bad chemistry phone call, nothing. Wait a bit, regain your composure and come back even more determined to succeed on the next call. The best way to overcome objections is to be more prepared. Create a paper trail for your explanations, and start with a letter. Build an outline of the points you need to make. Seek out the guidelines and add them to your outline or letter. Next, gather any documentation that will prove what you are trying to show. Example: If you say you are renting a room, then start making copies of the checks your receive for rent; if they pay cash, have them pay you by a money order, and start depositing into your account.

If they are using the wrong property value, make sure you are a few steps ahead by being prepared and doing your own research first. There are many free sites to get comparable property sales, build a sheet with three recently sold properties that are as close as possible to your home and as close to model matches. Verify cost per square foot.

Overcoming Bad Personalities

It is not your job to deal with rude people, and I do understand how difficult it is to be put into that situation. In addition, the thought of losing your home is extremely emotional, and most people tend to get defensive and very stressed out, especially in situations where they feel threatened. The key to all of this is being empowered, confident, and in control of your own file. Do not give away your power by losing control of your own emotions. I know that sometimes it is easier said than done. If you feel that you are not in a good place emotionally, then take a breather, go out for a walk and gain your inner peace before calling. DO not get into an argument, and do not get into a negative mode when speaking with anyone. It will only make things worse and will not get you anywhere. Keeping your cool is the key to success in every situation, even the loan modification process.

Affirmation:

I will be connected to the right representatives that will help me achieve a successful loan modification.

Affirmation:

At this moment, my loan modification is being worked up with the payment and terms that are right for me.

CHAPTER THREE

GETTING STARTED

I t's time to get ready. Here are some steps you can take to ensure a positive outcome:

Think Positive

◈ Without a positive attitude, it is difficult to get this done on your own.

◈ Be positive about your outcome and about preparing what you need to get approved for modification.

Commit to Making It Happen

◈ Commit to keeping your home and work hard at getting the job done.

◈ Be honest with yourself and ask, "How hard am I willing to work on this?" You need to be ready to fight for your home and not give up.

Stay Where You Are

◈ Do not move out of your house prematurely.

Approach Modification Like a Business

◈ Be calm. Taking the attitude that this is a job provides necessary distance from the situation.

Keep Your Emotions in Check

◈ You must try to separate yourself from some of

the emotions your situation may create. This will keep you sane and healthy.

Knowledge is Power

◊ This oft-used phrase says it best. Arm yourself with knowledge and information; this is essential to success.

Do Your Homework

◊ Know your rights as a mortgage holder.

◊ Understand the foreclosure process and what can and cannot happen.

◊ Know what you are talking about; know your situation inside and out before speaking with anyone.

◊ Ask questions.

> **To know where you are within the foreclosure timeline, see chart on pages 125 and 126**

Take Action, Get Organized, and Always be Prepared

◊ Keep copies of everything.

◊ Keep track of all follow-up tasks, such as items that need to be faxed, phone calls to make, notes to write.

◊ Read all correspondence you receive.

◊ Return phone calls and check your messages. Do

45

not let this frazzle you.

◊ Keep a log and take good notes.

Rethink Your Finances

◊ Consider any and all options you might have to improve your financial situation.

◊ Know your finances!

Beware of Scams

◊ You may receive letters in the mail that look official, or someone may knock on your door, but most of these are actually scams. If you look closely, these letters will state that they are advertisements and have no affiliation with your bank.

Have Patience

◊ The loan modification process can take time; you must be patient in order to get the answers you need.

Effectively and Efficiently Communicate With Your Lender

◊ Don't use profanity or be rude.

◊ Be assertive.

◊ Be prepared to call as many times as it takes and speak with supervisors to postpone any sale dates while you are processing/reprocessing your loan modification request.

◊ Escalate matters if you are not getting the attention you deserve.

GET READY. TAKE A DEEP BREATH. TAKE ACTION.

The worst thing you can do is to do nothing at all. **DON'T GIVE UP!**

Affirmation:

When I get out of my own way, magic and miracles assist me with difficulties with this loan modification.

CHAPTER FOUR

THE DIFFERENCE BETWEEN LOAN MODIFICATION AND FORBEARANCE

D o you know the difference between a loan modification and a forbearance?

This information is important, because many times the lender wants to push a forbearance on homeowners, when what you are requesting is a loan modification. Stand your ground, and if you have to, request to speak with a supervisor. Also, make sure you are talking to Loss Mitigation and not the Collections Department. They will remind you on every call that they are collectors. Their job is to try to collect as much as possible, and guess what? A forbearance does just that. It is the Collections Department that is trained to do this.

A Loan Modification Agreement is made between a mortgage lender and a delinquent borrower, in which the lender agrees not to exercise its legal right to foreclose on a mortgage. The borrower in turn agrees to MODIFY one or more terms of the original mortgage to make it more affordable, or save you from losing your home in the case of defaulted payments. This can include adding your past due payments to the end of the loan, lowering your interest rate, extending your mortgage term, i.e., from 30 to 40 years, deferring principal and not making it due until you either refinance, sell, or the term is up (usually with no interest or principal forgiveness (which is rare with most lenders), or any actual term change.

A Forbearance Agreement is not a loan modification. It is an agreement made between a mortgage lender and delinquent borrower, where the lender agrees not to exercise its legal right to foreclose on a mortgage, and the borrower agrees to a mortgage plan that will, over a certain time period, bring the borrower current on his or her payments. A forbearance agreement is not a long-term solution for delinquent borrowers; it is designed for borrowers who have temporary financial problems caused by unforeseen circumstances, such as loss of employment or health issues.

LOAN MODIFICATION VS. FORBEARANCE

	Dept. to Contact	Type of Solution	Reasons to Consider
Modification	Loss Mitigation	Long term	On-going financial problems due to change in circumstances
Forbearance	Collections	Short term	Temporary financial problems due to unforeseen circumstances

FYI: This is not a refinance

When your property value comes in lower than what you owe on your mortgage, it actually helps your numbers look better for loan modification purposes.

*Don't fight a low BPO/appraisal value.

CHAPTER FIVE

ORGANIZING YOUR DOCUMENTS

"Many can argue that reality is as it is, but my experience is that the opposite is exactly true, reality is ours for the making."
- Asara Lovejoy

I t is very important to be as organized as possible; both personally and with your information. You will need a way to assemble and store your documentation so it is readily available and easy to access.

Remember, you will be dealing with the Loss Mitigation Department, not with Collections, so you should have the correct contact information.

Supplies and Equipment

1. **Legal Size File Folder**
   ◊ This should contain important phone numbers, addresses, and fax numbers of your lender.

2. Legal Size Writing Paper

◈ Use this as a **CONVERSATION LOG**. Write down dates of your calls, as well as the dates you wrote to your lender or faxed them something. You need to know exactly who you spoke with, when, and what took place, and what paperwork you submitted.

◈ Staple this to one side of the legal size file folder.

3. Fax Machine

◈ Get a fax machine that you can connect to your phone line. This will save you the most money vs. paying for a monthly computer fax service. You should have a fax to send your lender documentation (usually many pages at a time and usually quite often). Save all of your fax confirmation pages.

4. Calculator

◈ You will need a calculator; preferably a mortgage calculator so you can calculate your income properly and add up your expenses correctly, as well as figure out mortgage payments based on certain rates the lender may offer you.

5. Calendar

◈ A calendar is necessary to note dates you need to follow up on tasks. As a reminder, **save copies of everything you submit with the date you sent it, and never send originals of your personal documents.**

Affirmation:

This loan modification challenge is an opportunity for greater success!

CHAPTER SIX

TRADITIONAL OR IN-HOUSE LOAN MODIFICATION PROGRAMS

A n in-house or traditional Loan Modification Program is usually calculated differently than the HAMP program calculations. It is best to call and see if you are able to get any information on the types of programs available and see if they will give you any of the guideline information on those programs. It is not likely that they will give you that information, but it's worth a try. You might not get everything, but asking might give you a glimpse into what's available.

Unless the program is a HAMP look-alike program, most of the "traditional" modifications are based on Income vs. Household expenses. It is difficult to guess exactly how their inside programs work, especially since you usually don't know how low they will go on the interest rate. However, we have been successful when working with our clients in helping them tighten up the household expense ship and lower as many expenses as possible to get them to an approximate positive number of $100 to $250.00. There might be times when a higher qualifying ratio is used; I have seen a 38% ratio used in some circumstances. The most used is the household income vs. expenses approach, which uses NET income, instead of the HAMP programs GROSS income calculation. Again, this really depends on the lender and the guidelines for the particular program. As the HAMP program gains momentum, they are only using the "traditional" or in-house programs when they cannot approve you for HAMP for any reason, when you are out of the parameters to be eligible for HAMP, or when your lender or investor does not participate in HAMP. Keep in mind that the calculations for this are VERY different than HAMP that uses only the 31% GROSS income and the expenses related only to the home such as the mortgage, interest, property taxes, homeowners insurance, and any homeowners association dues or fees.

As an example, net income $2,500.00

Total household expenses = $2,250, including mortgage property taxes, credit accounts, and household expenses, such as food, utilities, spending money, etc.

= $250.00 Surplus

ADVICE:

DON'T BE AFRAID TO ASK YOUR LENDER WHAT THEIR GUIDELINES ARE.

SECTION TWO

THE HOME AFFORDABLE MODIFICATION PROGRAM (HAMP)

CHAPTER SEVEN

ARE YOU A CANDIDATE FOR THE HOME AFFORDABLE MODIFICATION (HAMP) PROGRAM?

NOTE: Lenders/servicers usually offer more than one type of program and some "look" alike programs – make sure to ask what you're being qualified for and don't get discouraged!

DEFINITION

The President's plan was created to help homeowners experiencing hardships, such as:

◊ A rate increase

◊ Loss of employment

◊ Decreased income

◊ Increased expenses due to an illness or death in the family

With this program, you are able to get your payments more affordable, either through a refinance or a modification. For our purposes, we will only be discussing the modification option.

I would suggest that the first step to take is to find out whether your loan is Fannie Mae or Freddie Mac insured. This will help you to know if you fall under the guidelines of the government plan, Home Affordable Modification Program, abbreviated "HAMP." In addition, you can look up all of the guidelines for this program at their website, which is located at http://www.makinghomeaffordable.gov.

The Basics of the HAMP Program: Eligibility Rules

Below is the list of general eligibility criteria for the HAMP program:

- Your home must be your primary residence.
- The amount you owe on your first mortgage must be equal to or under $729,750.
- Your must have a financial hardship.
- Your mortgage must have been taken out before January 1, 2009.

Has your payment gone up, or your income gone down since you took out loan? OR, have you suffered a financial hardship, such as an increase in expenses from medical bills, divorce, etc.?

Is the payment on your current mortgage first loan (not including other mortgages) more than 31% of your GROSS (before taxes) income? **THE PAYMENT USED TO CALCULATE THIS IS PRINCIPAL, INTEREST,**

TAXES, INSURANCE, AND HOMEOWNER ASSOCIATION FEES.

Don't forget you need a calculator to get accurate figures!

If you answered "yes" to the five questions regarding eligibility and you know whether you are Fannie Mae or Freddie Mac, you will already know that you are either applying for the HAMP program or applying for another lender/investor program that is similar.

If it looks like you may be eligible for the HAMP program, call your lender and ask for **LOSS MITIGATION**. Tell them that you want to be considered for the Home Affordable Modification Program. Otherwise, let them know that you would like to submit a request for a modification under one of their programs.

My recommendation, if you are not out of time, is to fill out the Making Home Affordable RMA Application for HAMP, which is available at their website, http://www.makinghomeaffordable.gov, because as of June 1, 2010, this is a requirement of the program along with your financial checklist.

A Birds-Eye View: Behind the Scenes
The Loan Modification Process

BEHIND THE SCENES

1. ELIGIBILITY CRITERIA

2. MODIFIED PAYMENT CALCULATION

3. MODIFICATION TERMS

4. DOCUMENTATION

MODIFY LOAN

APPROVED!

Complexity of the Loan Modification Process:
Behind the Scenes From the FDIC

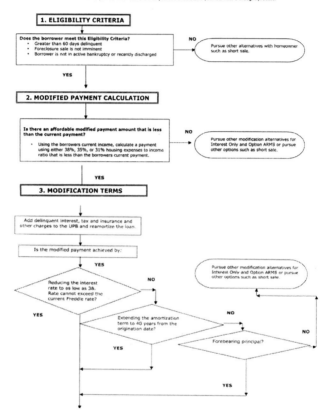

BEHIND THE SCENES
This is the flow chart the FDIC created to establish modification criteria. This is what your servicer uses as a guide to approve or deny your request. There are four parts to the chart: Eligibility Criteria, Modified Payment Calculation, Modification Terms, and Documentation. Familiarize yourself with this chart so you can understand your servicer's thought process.

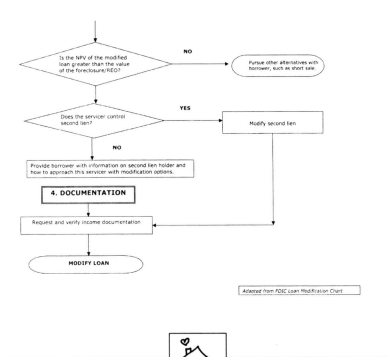

Adapted from FDIC Loan Modification Chart

Fannie or Freddie?

You will need to determine if either Fannie Mae or Freddie Mac insures your mortgage. Visit:

http://www.fanniemae.com/loanlookup/

or http://www.freddiemac.com/mymortgage

If your loan is not either Fannie or Freddie, do not fear! There are still many programs available from lenders. Some programs are even just as good and sometimes better, depending on your lender, servicer, or investor.

If your loan is indeed insured by Fannie or Freddie, then you will be able to figure out where you're at and what possibilities may be available to you.

BEFORE YOU CALL, GET THE LOAN MODIFICATION MINDSET

Next, go online to your lender's website and get all of the **LOSS MITIGATION** contact information (i.e., address, phone number, fax number) and their specific criteria for a loan modification request. Sometimes, you are able to upload and fill out information online, or via email, which is usually faster. If you don't have access to the Internet, call your lender and get the information from them directly. Shortly thereafter, you will be supplied with a list of the commonly requested documents. Your lender may require additional paperwork, but for the most part, this list will be the required documentation. Sometimes they don't need as much, but you are better off being prepared. Do not be afraid to ask your lender who your investor is, and if it is not Fannie or Freddie, then don't be afraid to ask them what programs are available to you and if they can tell you what the guidelines are for the available programs. This will give you a better understanding when you put your package together.

BEFORE YOU CALL YOUR LENDER ABOUT YOUR SPECIFIC LOAN SITUATION OR SCENARIO,

PLEASE MAKE SURE YOU HAVE READ THROUGH THIS SECTION AND HAVE PUT TOGETHER YOUR MODIFICATION REQUEST PACKAGE SO YOU ARE FULLY PREPARED AND CONFIDENT.

Be assertive when you contact your lender.

To Get Your

Comprehensive Do It Yourself System, visit:

www.theloanmodguru.com

SECTION THREE

MASTER YOUR POWER: SUBMITTING YOUR PACKAGE TO YOUR LENDER

CHAPTER EIGHT

ARE YOU PREPARED TO CONTACT YOUR LENDER?

I T IS BEST TO GATHER ALL OF YOUR INFORMATION AND DOCUMENTATION **BEFORE** CALLING YOUR LENDER. THIS WILL HELP REDUCE YOUR FRUSTRATION AND THE AMOUNT OF TIME IT TAKES, AND WILL HELP YOU FEEL CONFIDENT AND IN CONTROL OF YOUR SITUATION. IT WILL ALSO HELP THE LENDER BE ABLE TO OFFER YOU THE ASSISTANCE YOU NEED.

NOTE: Are you on a wage earner job or self employed? Depending on this, you will need certain documents for everyone listed on the loan.

Things to Think About While Preparing Your Package

Are you ready to give up certain expenses that are unnecessary?

Are you willing to take on an extra part-time job, rent a room out, or turn a passion of yours into some extra side money? These are some items you will want to cover after you look at your financial "big" picture.

Start thinking of ways to do the above, as it may be necessary to consider if your lender declines you the first time. Do not give up. Find ways to make it work and stay positive.

Even if you get a negative person on the other side of the line, keep on going. **DO NOT GIVE UP**; send them blessings and move on until you get the right helpful person on the other end. If all else fails, mail an escalation letter until you get someone at the top to listen to you. This is exactly the scenario where you **MUST** be the squeaky wheel, but be a nice squeaky wheel. Still, be assertive and know your stuff.

IF YOU KNOW YOU CAN MAKE A REASONABLE PAYMENT AND YOU WANT TO STAY IN YOUR HOME, GO ALL THE WAY! Write down your goal. Look at it and repeat to yourself that you are going to accomplish this. See it as already being approved.

If you know that there is no way you can make any payment of even a reasonable payment, then you should look at other options, but **ALWAYS** make an attempt to save your home. If you are just going to have to pay rent somewhere else, then you should make every effort to keep your home; you may be very pleased with the results. Sometimes the modified payments are exactly what you needed, but you will never know if you do not move forward and take action.

> **Mindset, determination, and the belief that you will succeed are the most important characteristics to accomplish your loan modification. Be prepared to let nothing get in the way of saving your home.**

How to Accurately Calculate Your Debt to Income Ratio (DTI) With Income Calculation Explanation

Whether you think you make too much or too little, you must have an accurate picture of your finances when applying for loan modification. A big part of this is properly calculating your income. The reason why this is so important is because servicers look at your wages to mortgage ratio. This ratio looks at ALL of the costs involved with holding a mortgage such as principal, interest, taxes and insurance. Your income number is based on your GROSS monthly income, before any deductions (taxes, FSA's, etc). Lenders use the wage to mortgage ratio to make sure you can afford your house and mortgage payments every month.

To get started, you will need to gather some information:

- Your most recent home tax bill
- Principal and interest statement from your lender
- Homeowner's insurance policy and bill
- Most recent paycheck stubs or previous year's tax returns
- W-2's, 1099's

Step One:

Add up your yearly total of the home tax bill and the homeowner's insurance bill. Divide this number by 12 to provide you with a monthly amount of taxes and insurance.

For example, let's say your yearly tax bill is $2,400 and your homeowner's insurance is $1,200. $3,600 divided by 12 = $300.00 a month.

Step Two:

Find your principal and interest statement from your lender. The monthly breakdown is usually already calculated for you. Note the monthly interest charges.

For example, let's say your monthly mortgage payment is $1,850, with $800 going to principal, and $1,050 going to interest.

Step Three – Determining Your Income:

For people who receive paychecks and W-2's:

Get your paycheck stubs, W-2's, or last year's income tax returns. You need to calculate your gross monthly income based on this information. Also, remember this is before taxes or any other deductions. If your paycheck is prepared by payroll, it will usually have a "YTD Earnings" section. Also, note the "Paid-To-Date" on the check stub, as this will help you determine how many months the yearly amount applies to.

Examples to help determine your monthly income:

If you have your YTD info:

When paid thru 4/21, divide 21 (number of days you have been paid for in the month) x 30 (number of days in that particular month) to get correct ratio .7 +3 months = 3.7

Example: $2,000 YTD thru 4/21 paycheck

$2,000/3.7= $540.54 per month

W2 employees:

Calculating wages also add: YTD

Example: When paid thru 4/21, divide 21 x 30 to get correct ratio .7 plus 3 months 3.7

Example: $2,000 YTD thru 4/21 paycheck

$2,000/3.7= $540.54 per month

OR

Paid on 15th and 30th

Take this gross wage amount X 24 then /divide by 12 to get monthly

OR

Paid bi-weekly (every 2 weeks on different dates)

Take this gross wage amount X 26 then /divide by 12 to get monthly wage

OR

Paid weekly

Take this gross wage amount X by 52 then /divide by 12 to get monthly gross wage

Non taxable income, ie: Social Security

Gross up by 125%

Example $1,000.00 x 125% = $1,250.00/month income for the purpose of mortgage wage calculation.

Rental Income: Lenders use 75% of the total - please see rental income explanation.

If you are self-employed, you will need to prove sufficient income that will be verified via:

- 1099's
- Profit and Loss - NET income after expenses is used as GROSS for HAMP and most in-house programs.
- Bank statements that show deposits at the start of the gross on your Profit and Loss statement. This is a backup that the lender may ask for, so just plan on having it ready and available.

*See reference section for Profit & Loss example and Bank Statement Analysis.

Step Four:

Add your monthly mortgage tax + insurance + principal + interest. This is your total monthly mortgage obligation.

Using our example:

Tax + Insurance: $300/month
Principal + Interest: $1,850/month
Your total monthly mortgage obligation would be $2,150.

Step Five:

To calculate your wage to mortgage ratio, you need to divide your monthly mortgage obligation ($2,150) by your monthly gross income (for example, $4,166) = 0.5160

Take this number and multiply it times 100 to get the percentage of your monthly gross income that you need for your monthly mortgage obligation:

0.5160 x 100 = 51.6%

51.6% of $4166 = $2,149, which is right where your monthly mortgage obligations are.

If you make less than this, you would need to show other income. If you made more than this, up to a certain point, you would need to show other expenses, which is discussed in greater detail in the book.

Step Six:

Housing DTI = House Payment /divided by Gross Monthly Household Income = Front-End DTI Ratio.

Total DTI = Monthly Debt Payments /divided by Gross Monthly Household Income = Back-End DTI Ratio.

PERFECT NUMBER: 38% DTI is the magic number that most lenders want you to have for most in-house loan modification programs, 31% ONLY for the housing ratio or Front End ratio for HAMP or HAMP look alikes. They use the back end to calculate if you are over 55% total DTI to refer you to the HUD approved credit counselor.

But, it is possible get approved at ratios 31+ to 78% on other programs, and many of those programs use net income vs. expenses or Total Back End Ratios.

How will I know if I need to "lower" my DTI?

If you've got over a 55% DTI, it's a good idea to be smart to try to "fix" or consolidate some of your debt that is on your credit report – more than likely you will be asked to speak with a HUD approved credit counselor before being approved for a government loan modification i.e., car loan, the credit card debt, etc.

QUICK DTI FIXERS: If you have saved up money, you can use your cash on hand to pay off your car loan or trade for one without a payment. With this, you have reduced $200-600 off you're the TOTAL monthly debt, and you'll be a much better candidate for a modification.

NOTE: Keep in mind that your lender, servicer, or investor may change guidelines or programs over time, and many of the different lenders have different targets for DTI and limitations on what they will approve.

Affirmation:
I am so happy now that my mortgage payment will be _____ (fill in the blank, reasonably.)

Affirmation:
I have the power to handle success with my loan modification.

Contacting Loss Mitigation Before You Start: Loan Modification Survival Strategies of the Fittest

It should be a number one priority for you to take great care of yourself. Give yourself time to walk in nature, do breathing exercises, listen to calming music, etc. If you don't take care of yourself, your stress can make you sick, and you should also know this stress is passed on to your family. I cannot tell you enough how important this piece of advice is. I know that the kind of stress you are going through can eat you up and spit you out. You can suffer from extreme anxiety to extreme depression. The nightmare feelings and emotions you feel with the threat of foreclosure are not fun and games. It can destroy families, cause job loss, divorces, and drinking

73

problems, as well as scar your children for a long time. Don't lose the perspective that NOTHING, not even a house, is as important to you as the well-being and happiness of you and your family. Don't let anything make you a victim because the only way that you can be a victim is if you let this situation get to you.

Stand up and fight, fight as a family, give it your best and your all with a positive attitude. With a positive attitude and determination, along with your faith in the Lord, you can do anything, even move mountains. If, in the end, you still have your health and your family and YOU decide after going for this all the way that YOU chose to take other options, then there are millions of other houses out there. So don't lose your sanity and family over a house. I am not saying not to fight for your home or that it is not important to you, because I know it is, but give it its own place in the scheme of things.

It is okay to admit that something significant has taken place in your life. Then you can confront your fears and begin to take action with a new perspective and courage.

Put your focus on the good times; don't dwell on the negatives, as it takes time for the process. During this process, you have to see that God has something bigger and better planned and remind yourself that, no matter what happens, you will be victorious.

Be open to change, as it is a time to invest in your self-development, do the things you dream about, reinvent yourself, learn new things, focus on the positive things in life, read good books, and listen to motivational stories. Find things that make you feel alive and bring that life to everything you do.

Take things only one day at a time, while remembering you are never alone. Tomorrow will be the first of many new days, filled with new opportunities for success, so don't worry about tomorrow. Live in the moment; be present in your life. Show up for your life every day.

Count your blessings every day, as well, as many times a day as possible. Keep a positive outlook. Be patient, yet determined and relentless, in the process, but always approach it with an attitude of gratitude and positive energy for all you with whom you come into contact.

Be persistent with what you want to happen. Be unstoppable; don't give up. Take notes. Take names, ask for supervisors, get your sale postponed, and if you are at that point, keep calling until you get someone who will listen and do something about it.

Learn as much as you can about the process. If you want to do this on your own, you have to do it as a professional would. Gain the knowledge. Read articles. Learn the lingo. Become familiar with your lender. Ask them about their programs. If you happen to get an unpleasant, or even downright mean person on the other end, call again until you find a helpful one, and send those positive thoughts to every single one of them; they are stressed, too.

By following the above survival strategies for loan modification, you will find yourself more successful at everything you do in life.

Affirmation:

I embody love, success, and happiness at every moment and in every situation.

Affirmation:

I appreciate the way this condition helps me understand more clearly what I want in life.

REMEMBER: When calling in, make sure you are speaking to Loss Mitigation vs. Collections. The collection department has one goal: COLLECTING (like the recording says)

How is Your Income Calculated When Qualifying for a Loan Modification?

Your monthly income is your gross pay prior to any deductions made through payroll. They will calculate your wage or your salary based on numbers that include any overtime you receive, commission you make, tips or bonuses you get, allowances for housing, and will include any other payments you get for the service you provide.

If you know you will lose or gain a certain income benefit in the very near future or already have and you need this to be calculated for your approval, prepare yourself with a letter from your employer that clearly states the date these changes will take place.

If you receive any Social Security payments either for yourself or a minor, or have insurance payments made to you or annuity payments, pension income, retirement income, unemployment insurance income or other benefits, such as disability or death benefits, this income will be used, as well, with the proper proof. If this income is not taxable, they will multiply this income by 125% to get to the correct monthly gross income.

Child and alimony support payments can also be used if you can prove this income.

Calculate rental income at 75% of the total amount, as they give 25% as a maintenance and vacancy factor. Be sure you are not hit twice for some expenses.

If you are self employed when you provide your profit and loss, make sure they are not counting the same expense from the profit and loss AND your credit report. When every dollar counts for your approval, the best practice is to verify every number, line by line, to ensure accuracy on the part of your servicer.

Be prepared to challenge the numbers. Self-employed income is calculated for HAMP using the NET from your submitted profit and loss statement. Be prepared with bank statements that back up these numbers.

If you voluntarily provide income from household sources for people that are not on your loan, but who contribute to your household, such as boarder income (room rental), the servicer should include it as long as you have documentation and verifiable proof that you can rely on this income to be used by you to support the mortgage payment. The servicer will use this income and calculate it in the same manner as they calculate your income. You do not have to worry, just because they use this income, it does not mean that the other person will now be liable for your loan, nor will it be on their credit.

After your initial trial period, the servicer will re-verify your most current income documentation to make sure the changes are not more than a 25% difference from the pretrial numbers. If there is a 25% or greater difference, you will have to start a whole new trial period and be reevaluated for eligibility for the Home Affordable Modification Program, as required by the program guidelines. If your income changes, you must be prepared to restart the program trial.

Alimony, Separation Maintenance, and Child Support Income

Borrowers are not required to use alimony, separation maintenance, or child support income to qualify for HAMP. However, if the borrower chooses to provide this income, it should be documented with (i) copies of the divorce decree, separation agreement, or other legal written agreement filed with a court, or a court decree that provides for the payment of alimony or child support and states the amount of the award and the period of time over Supplemental Directive 10-01 Page 5 which it will be received, and (ii) evidence of receipt of payment, such as copies of the two most recent bank statements or deposit advices showing deposit amounts. If the borrower voluntarily provides such income, and that income renders the borrower ineligible for a HAMP offer, the servicer is allowed to remove that income from consideration and re-evaluate the borrower for HAMP eligibility.

Income Checklist

Gather the following information for yourself and any co-borrowers:

◊ The last two (2) years' tax returns

◊ W2's

◊ IRS Form 4506T for the lender to request a transcript from the IRS to match your returns

◊ One full month of most recent paycheck stubs

◊ If you are self employed, three (3) months' most recent Profit and Loss (P&L) statement. Some lenders may request the full year to date P&L and bank statements. *See Reference Section P&L example.

◊ Gather your income from all sources, e.g., room rental, SSI, or family contributions)

◊ Keep copies of checks people pay you with.

◊ If you receive room rents or have rental property, then you will need a copy of the rental agreement. Be prepared if the lender wants you to provide copies as proof for any rents received.

◊ If you have household contributions made by others, get letters signed by the contributor saying how much they give you and be prepared to submit if the bank needs proof.

◊ MAKE COPIES OF CHECKS BEFORE CASHING. The lender may request a Schedule E and usually will for rental properties.

◊ Two (2) full months of bank statements, or four (4) months if you are self employed.

◊ Copy of your most current first mortgage payment coupon or statement.

◊ Copy of your most current statement from your second mortgage loan, if you have one.

◊ Your most recent property tax statement.

◊ Your current homeowner's insurance declaration page.

◊ Your most recent homeowner's association bill (if applicable).

◊ A recent utility bill (for proof of residency).

Take the guesswork out and find out how HAMP calculates your income at www.theloanmodguru.com

What About My Credit?
How Loan Modification Affects Your Credit Report

As part of your modification tasks, you must submit a request for a credit hold.

What is a Credit Hold?

A credit hold stops the bank from reporting your credit status while your modification application is being processed. This can be very beneficial, as it stops any negative information from being submitted to the three credit reporting agencies. You will need to write a brief letter to your lender requesting the credit hold, and send copies to the attention of both the credit reporting department and the executive offices. While it is at the lender's discretion to honor your request, it is absolutely worth your while.

Once your permanent loan modification has been approved, you need to check with all of the credit reporting agencies and review for any errors on the reports.

How your modification gets reported if you are late delinquent or late on payments

If a homeowner enters into the modification trial period, but has been late on mortgage payments, the servicer will most likely report the mortgage as what is referred to as a "30-day late." Most lenders use a three-month trial period, where the homeowner must make the proposed new modification mortgage payment amount on time. If the homeowner fulfils the responsibilities of the trial period, he or she will be offered a permanent modification.

In terms of credit reporting, homeowners are noted as being "delinquent" during the trial period because the proposed loan modification amount is less than the actual monthly mortgage payment and because this trial period is NOT recognized as being accepted/permanent. Because the trial payment is not the total payment, it is viewed as a partial payment, resulting in a 30-day late being reported each month during the trial period.

If your loan is owned or guaranteed by Fannie Mae, see page 12 of Fannie Mae Servicing Guide Announcement 09-05R for information about credit reporting for HAMP-modified Fannie Mae loans, where it states:

"If a borrower is current when they enter the Trial Period, the servicer should report the borrower current but on a modified payment if the borrower makes timely payments by the last business day of each Trial Period month at the modified amount during the Trial Period. If a borrower is delinquent when they enter the Trial

Period, the servicer should continue to report in such a manner that accurately reflects the borrower's delinquency and workout status following usual and customary reporting standards. In both cases, the servicer should report the modification when it becomes final."

If your loan is owned or guaranteed by Freddie Mac, see page 5 of Freddie Mac Publication 800 for servicer instructions re: credit reporting of modified loans, where it states:

"Borrowers who are current when they enter into the Trial Period and make payments by the 30th day of each month, report as current, but on a modified payment. Borrowers who are delinquent when they enter into the Trial Period or do not make payments by the 30th of each month, report according to borrower's delinquency and workout status. Notify when borrowers have completed the modification."

If your loan is NOT owned or guaranteed by Fannie Mae or Freddie Mac, see page 22 of "HAMP Servicer Supplemental Directive 09-01" for information about credit reporting guidelines for modified non-GSE loans. It specifies the following:

"The servicer should continue to report a "full-file" status report to the four major credit repositories for each loan under the HAMP...on the basis of the following: (i) for borrowers who are current when they enter the trial period, the servicer should report the borrower current but on a modified payment if the borrower makes timely payments by the 30th day of each trial period month at the modified amount during the trial period, as well as report the modification when completed, and (ii) for borrowers who are delinquent when they enter the trial period, the servicer should continue to report in such a manner that accurately reflects the borrower's delinquency and workout status following usual and customary reporting standards, as well as report the modification when completed. More detailed guidance on these reporting requirements will be published by the CDIA."

Some servicers tell homeowners they are required by the Treasury Dept. to report in this manner, while others will tell the homeowner that they are being reported as "late" in an effort to separate people who are actually able to afford their mortgages vs. those who truly need modification.

Homeowners who were delinquent when they entered the modification trial period, however, will continue to be reported as delinquent during the trial period.

How your modification gets reported if you are NOT late on payments

Homeowners who are current on their mortgage payments when they enter into the trial modification period should NOT be reported as late. This is stated in the guidelines for Fannie Mae, Freddie Mac and other loans being modified by HAMP-participating services. Make sure your lender is accurately reporting you.

How can I keep my credit score from being damaged while applying for a modification?

The best thing to do is to apply for modification while your mortgage is current, continue to make payments, and work to get into the trial period as quickly as possible. Remember, you do not have to be behind on mortgage payments to apply for modification!

What should I do if I have already applied for loan modification?

Contact your lender to find out how your account is being reported to the credit agencies. Clear up any discrepancies before you enter the trial period. If need be, fax, mail and call your lender with the appropriate HAMP guidelines as they may feign ignorance!

What happens when I enter into a permanent modification at a lower payment?

When you enter into a permanent loan modification, your servicer will report your loan as "current, but on a modified amount." How will this affect your credit? While reporting agencies do no publish their scoring calculations, the hit in your credit score will not be as severe as multiple 30-day late, another reason to get through the trial period (while keeping your mortgage current) and into permanent modification as quickly as you can.

What if my modification is not through HAMP?

The guidelines for Fannie Mae and Freddie Mac listed above, are HAMP-specific. If you have a non-HAMP modification application—possibly an in-house modification, etc.—the credit reporting guidelines do not apply. In this scenario, you will have to negotiate how your account is reported as part of your modification process. If the lender states they will report negatively on you, you should take this into consideration when trying to modify your mortgage.

*Reminder, you do not have to be behind on mortgage payments to apply for modification; however, if you are not in imminent default. Please visit the "Imminent Default" section for more information.

The author has made every effort to provide the most accurate internet addresses and phone numbers to resources at the time of publication and neither publisher nor author assumes any responsibility for errors or changes that occur after the publication of this book and the author is not responsible for any content from these resources.

LOAN MODIFICATION PROCESS FOR PEOPLE WHO ARE NOT LATE: HAMP or Other Programs

This is the formula used when you are not currently in default to determine whether or not your default is imminent:

The borrower's debt coverage ratio is less than 1.20. The debt coverage ratio is the borrower's monthly disposable net income divided by the borrower's current monthly principal and interest payment on the first lien mortgage loan (excluding tax and insurance payments). Monthly disposable net income is the borrower's monthly gross income less (1) monthly payroll deductions, (2) monthly escrow allocations of property taxes, property insurance, and mortgage insurance premiums, (3) monthly homeowner's or condominium association fees, (4) monthly allocations of all other monthly credit obligations, (5) all other reasonable living expenses allocated monthly, and (6) any other monthly net negative amounts paid or incurred by borrower (such as negative rental income, mortgage loan payments on investment properties); and the borrower's cash reserves are less than three times the current monthly mortgage payment, including tax and insurance payments (using estimated payments if the mortgage loan is not currently escrowed). Cash reserves are liquid assets the borrower has available for withdrawal from any financial institution or brokerage firm, including checking and savings accounts, certificates of deposit (even if held for an extended time), mutual funds, money market funds, stocks, or bonds.

CHAPTER NINE

EXPENSES

IF YOU HAVE NEVER DONE THIS BEFORE, IT IS A REAL EYE OPENER. SEEING WHAT YOUR MONTHLY EXPENSES ARE VS. YOUR INCOME OFTEN UNCOVERS A NEED TO BUCKLE DOWN ON EXPENSES!

Make a list of your average monthly expenses for each of the following items:

◈ Household Expenses (groceries, cleaning supplies, clothing, etc.)

◈ Credit Card Balances (minimum payment)

◈ Student Loans

◈ Auto Loans, Lines of Credit

◈ Utilities

◈ Medical Insurance

◈ Medical Expenses (medicine, co-pays, anything not covered by health insurance)

◈ Car Insurance

Once you have all of this information, you are ready to put your financial worksheet together.

Do not call your lender until you are completely prepared, but don't take a long time to get your documents ready—the sooner, the better.

IMPORTANT: If you are in jeopardy of a trustee sale date, **YOU MUST ACT QUICKLY TO POSTPONE IT; OTHERWISE, YOU WILL LOSE YOUR HOME. IN THIS CASE, SUBMIT YOUR PACKAGE FOR REVIEW AS SOON AS POSSIBLE!**

The Hardship Letter

You will need to write a hardship letter that clearly outlines your change in circumstances. By writing the letter, you will help your lender see and understand your personal situation. It is important to take sufficient time to write an effective letter.

What is Hardship?

Your hardship letter should explain what has happened that has made it impossible for you to continue paying your mortgage at its present amount/rate. An example of a hardship letter can be found below, and it is also included in the **Reference** section of this book.

Make a list of all of the reasons your financial situation has changed and plan out the letter:

◇ What are the specifics of your situation?

◇ Is it based on financial pressure?

◇ What challenges are you facing?

◇ Medical issues?

◇ Job loss for you or your household?

◇ When did the hardship begin? Is it temporary or permanent and why?

Include ideas you have to improve your situation:

◇ What are you doing to make things better?

◇ How is this situation going to change, i.e., looking for a new job, increasing income, trying to rent a room?

Have a clear introduction so that the person opening the letter understands what you need and gets your request to the right place.

◇ If you know how much you can afford, let them know.

◇ Reiterate your desire to stay in your home and keep your property.

◇ Be concise—not more than one page.

◇ Be specific and to the point, but also let them know what this stress is doing to you and that you want to work with them to find solutions so you can stay in your home.

◇ All borrowers will need to sign and date the hardship letter.

**Hardship Letter
Templates are available
online at
www.theloanmodguru.com**

How to Deal With People
at the Bank

If you call your bank and the person on the line is rude or unpleasant, you can always **politely** listen to what they have to say. **DON'T TAKE IT PERSONALLY,** get the information you need, and then finish the call. If necessary, you can always call again at another time and hope you'll get someone nicer. Bear in mind, sometimes these people have issues going on in their own lives, too. Just move on, and **DON'T LET YOURSELF GET WORKED UP AND FRUSTRATED.**

REMEMBER, YOU SIGNED UP TO TAKE THIS ON AND SOMETIMES THIS IS PART OF THE DEAL. DO NOT LET ANYONE DISRUPT YOUR INNER PEACE.

You are on a mission. Do not forget your goals and sense of purpose, regardless what anyone tells you! Don't forget who you are! You can do this!

SECTION FOUR

HOLD THEM ACCOUNTABLE TO TRANSPARENCY: KEEPING TRACK OF YOUR HAMP PROGRESS WITH YOUR LENDER

CHAPTER TEN

DETAILS TO REMEMBER AND BASIC CRITERIA

W rite your loan number on everything and be organized.

Always write your **LOAN NUMBER** on **EVERY** single piece of paper you submit to the lender and never send your original documentation to them. Lost faxes are the biggest triggers of frustration for borrowers. Know this in advance and then you have an advantage.

Verify Contact Information and Receipt

Before you start sending and faxing all of your information, call your lender and verify that the contact numbers, addresses, etc., are all correct for **LOSS MITIGATION**.

Call your lender to verify the receipt of your application. It can take 24 to 72 hours for information to be uploaded to their system. CALL, CALL, CALL to make sure they have it.

Note all dates on your calendar—when you sent your application, when you called and verified that it was received, etc. Stay conscious of any dates, such as a Trustee sale and follow up to make sure that those things that need to get postponed are postponed.

Show Adequate Income

Only your lender can tell you if you qualify, based on the characteristics of your loan and criteria for meeting requirements for modification. This is why it is so important that you are able to show that you have adequate income to be able to make the modified payment, but there are other items the lender will consider.

Always Be on Top of the Situation

Stay on top of your file. Unfortunately, this is your fight, so you have to hold yourself responsible to call and check on the status of your application. Regardless of how long it takes your lender to input the application and start processing it, you need to be certain you are not declined without being notified while your house gets sold at Trustee sale just because you didn't check on the progress of your case.

Affirmation:
Only knowledgeable bank representatives are working on my loan modification approval.

Affirmation:
I am thrilled that the negotiator assigned to me is so wonderful.

Ask Questions

You must keep asking questions. Go to the lender's websites to read their loss mitigation checklist and information. Ask your lender why and how so you can get familiar with what changes you need to make to be able to qualify for a loan modification.

Again, if you are denied, find out exactly why. Go back to your income and expenses to see what you need to change in your finances, whether it is a decrease in expenses or increasing your income.

Be Patient

Be patient as this process can take one to six months, **AND** sometimes more if the lender is overwhelmed with applications. Always consider the fact that your servicer or lender may not be the actual investor on **YOUR LOAN**. The majority of loans are sold to different investors, and sometimes the company servicing your loan stays the same; this is why you don't really know if they are your investor.

The Process According to HAMP

When you submit your modification package, you will often receive an acknowledgement letter like the one below. It will confirm the receipt of your application, explain the evaluation process and that while your home may be in foreclosure, a foreclosure sale will not occur during this evaluation period.

EXHIBIT B:
MODEL LETTER FOR SIMULTANEOUS TRIAL PLAN:
FORECLOSURE PROCESS EXPLANATION

[Servicer Logo] [Date] [Name] [Address 1] [Address 2]

Dear [borrower and co-borrower name(s)]:

We are committed to helping you retain your home. That's why we are currently evaluating your mortgage for eligibility in the Home Affordable Modification Program ("HAMP"), which would modify the terms of your loan and make your mortgage payments more affordable. Your loan has been previously referred to foreclosure, and we will continue the foreclosure process while we evaluate your loan for HAMP. However, no foreclosure sale will be conducted and you will not lose your home during the HAMP evaluation.

HAMP Eligibility

If you are eligible for HAMP, you will enter into a "trial period." You will receive a Trial Period Plan Notice, which will contain a new trial payment amount (this will temporarily replace your current mortgage payment during the HAMP trial period). To accept the Trial Period Plan, you must make your first trial payment by the specified due date. Once you accept, we will halt the foreclosure process as long as you continue to make your required trial plan payments.

If you do not qualify for HAMP, or if you fail to comply with the terms of the Trial Period Plan, you will be sent a Non-Approval Notice. In most cases, you will have 30 days to review the reason for non-approval and contact us to discuss any concerns you may have. During this

97

30-day review period, we may continue with the pending foreclosure action, but no foreclosure sale will be conducted and you will not lose your home.

Important—Do not ignore any foreclosure notices.

The HAMP evaluation and the process of foreclosure may proceed at the same time. You may receive foreclosure/eviction notices - delivered by mail or in person - or you may see steps being taken to proceed with a foreclosure sale of your home. While you will not lose your home during the HAMP evaluation, to protect your rights under applicable foreclosure law, you may need to respond to these foreclosure notices or take other actions. If you have any questions about the foreclosure process and the evaluation of your HAMP request, contact us at [XXX.XXX.XXXX]. If you do not understand the legal consequences of the foreclosure, you are also encouraged to contact a lawyer or housing counselor for assistance.

Questions

Call XXX.XXX.XXXX if you cannot afford to make your trial period payments, but want to remain in your home. Or if you have decided to leave your home, contact us— we have other options that may be able to help you avoid foreclosure. Additionally, if you have any questions about the foreclosure (or other legal notices that you receive), please call us for assistance. You can also call the Homeowner's HOPE™ Hotline at 1-888-995-HOPE (4673) if you need further counseling. They offer free HUD-certified counseling services in English and Spanish, and can help answer any questions you have.

> There are NO grace period days for trial modifications, i.e., the normal 15 days that a lender usually gives you.

Affirmation:

My bank is the leader in assisting people like me to have affordable mortgage payments, and they are working on my perfect loan modification solution.

The 3-Month Wait

Although it can indeed take up to six months, lending companies are currently taking approximately 90 days to decide if it will agree to its borrower's loan modification. What should you do during this often excruciating waiting period? You should take action.

Many of us fail to plan for the future. In fact, that could be why you are in your current situation. The good news is that you have the ability right now to stop responding to life and start charting your course, even if that course includes foreclosure.

Day 1

You submitted all the paperwork for the loan modification yesterday. Today, determine what options you can choose should you fail to get approval for the modification. Some options may be getting another job, selling your home, modifying your standard of living, selling gas-guzzling vehicles, renting out a room in your home or allowing the bank to foreclose on your home. Ask a trusted, unbiased friend to look over your choices and determine if you are missing any alternatives.

Day 7

Determine your priorities. Now that you know the choices available to you, you and your significant other must do serious soul-searching. Take this week to individually list the top 10 must-haves in your list of life. **Advice:** Be brutally honest and don't keep something off the list because you feel guilty for wanting it. If you lie and the worst-case scenario happens, resentment for unfilled expectations is the last thing you need. Some priorities may be maintaining a high standard of dress, stopping foreclosure at all costs, ensuring the children remain in private school, living in the same geographical area of the city, maintaining a strong marriage, ensuring the children continue in extracurricular activities.

Call your lender and check to see if they have received all the documents.

Day 14

Hopefully your list is well marked with strikeouts and eraser marks. If it's not, determine if you've really wrestled with this exercise. Set a time with your mate this week to discuss your lists together. Suggestions:

1. Do it in a public place, such as a coffee house, to ensure you both maintain self-control.

2. Plan for differences of opinion; walk in expecting your lists to deviate greatly.

3. The first thing you should do immediately after you sit down is write out what you agree to do and not do when you have conflicts on the list. Some agreements might be: promising to hear the other's point entirely before you engage in commenting on the priority, not saying anything about the differing priority until a few days have passed, or purposing to truly seek out the motivations behind the priority. For instance, a woman may not want to give up her desire for fashion labels. Initially, this may seem shallow to her man; however, if he truly understands her upbringing and work environment, he may see there are justifiable reasons for this being one of her priorities. Give your lists two weeks to air out.

Don't forget to call your lender to check the status.

Day 28

If Day 14's exercise was particularly volatile, but if maintaining a strong love relationship was on both of your lists, then you might consider calling a counselor who specializes in conflict resolution this week. Honestly, most of us have never been taught how to handle conflict in a healthy way. Seeing a conflict resolution specialist will probably be the best thing you could choose through this entire process. Don't let cost be an issue: Many companies have student interns whose fees are greatly reduced. Humble yourself and get over the age issue—these guys went to school for counseling. They know more than you do. Still resistant to counseling? Answer this: What's the point of saving your home if there won't be content bodies to share it?

If both did okay in discussing your lists, get together this week and determine what will be on your top 10 list as a couple.

On this date, call your lender to check status and prepare to get updated documents.

Affirmation:

The universe has my back for my greatest success with my loan modification.

Affirmation:

My loan modification is resolving easily and effortlessly, even as I speak.

SECTION FIVE

GOOD NEWS: MISSION ACCOMPLISHED

THE TRIAL OR PERMANENT MODIFICATION APPROVAL

CHAPTER ELEVEN

CONGRATULATIONS: YOU'VE BEEN APPROVED!

This is good news.

W hen you receive your modification approval, please make sure you carefully review it. If you do not understand the language, seek professional assistance. It is very important to follow all instructions. Call your lender if you need clarification.

IF YOU HAVE ANY DISCREPANCIES FROM WHAT THEY TOLD YOU OR WHAT YOU CALCULATED, CALL AND VERIFY THE INCOME AND EXPENSES THEY USED ARE CORRECT.

Check what needs to be filled out and if a notary is required, go get the documents notarized. **Advice:** Quite often, there is a notary at your bank or mail/shipping store who can do this for you at a nominal fee.

Modification Approval Checklist

◊ Check the date your approval acceptance needs to be received by the lender.

◊ Check to see if you need to send back any payment with the modification.

◊ Verify addresses, amounts and dates.

◈ Send a cashier's check/money order and also send cashier's checks/money orders for your trial payments. The last thing a bank wants to see is a bounced check during your trial period.

◈ Verify, verify, verify. Call and check the receipt of your modification acceptance documents and payments.

◈ For HAMP you will have three trial payments before you have a permanent modification, as this is what the guidelines for the program require.

◈ Make sure you have a modification, not just a forbearance, which is only temporary. This is different than the HAMP program trial modification. Some lenders will require a three-month forbearance trial while processing your modification request. This is good, especially if you are in jeopardy of a foreclosure sale because this will stop it.

KEEP CHECKING YOUR DATES FROM THE NOTICE OF TRUSTEE SALE. CALL THE SALE LINE. SOMETIMES MISTAKES ARE MADE. KEEP FOLLOWING UNTIL YOUR PERMANENT MODIFICATION IS IN HAND AND SEE THAT THE SALE IS CANCELLED VS. POSTPONED.

VERIFY the terms of the modification and follow up to make sure the lender uploads the terms of the new loan modification into the system. This can be quick OR can be another nightmare. FOLLOW UP AND ESCALATE, IF NECESSARY.

I GOT MY LOAN MODIFICATION, NOW WHAT?

Should I keep my home - or rent?

Great tools and calculators are available at this Freddie Mac website:

http://www.freddiemac.com/corporate/buyown/english/calcs_tools/

Check out your benefits, including:

Rent vs. Buy: Understand the financial differences between renting and homeownership.

Tax Savings: Learn about the potential tax savings with homeownership.

Affirmation:

I am an ever-expanding being of Power,
and I am succeeding with my loan modification that is
perfect for me.

Affirmation:

I know that life is planning only great things for me; it is
happening already.

SECTION SIX

I NEED A MIRACLE: HELP! I'VE BEEN DENIED, AND I DON'T WANT TO LOSE MY HOME!

CHAPTER TWELVE

SPECIFICS:

HAMP Requirements for Modification Approval

T rying to navigate the tedious job of modifying your own loan is frustrating enough. Find some time to sit in silence and regroup your inner peace; then you will have the strength within to carry on and be successful with your goals, while maintaining a positive outlook and attitude.

Patience is important, and I want to prepare you for the possibility of being denied. Even if this happens, you can find out why with the recent changes (as of 1/1/2010) to HAMP. The servicer MUST tell you why you were denied; with this information, you can make the necessary changes and reapply.

STEP ONE:

HOW YOUR MODIFICATION ELIGIBILITY IS CALCULATED

Your total GROSS (before taxes) income multiplied by 31%. This is called your DTI, or Debt to Income Ratio. BE CAREFUL: You must provide the servicer with your current income, which could potentially show a decrease; otherwise, they will use a previous year's tax return, where your income may have been higher. If there is any discrepancy, you will need to fight this.

Note: 31% = the modified payment amount including principal, interest, property taxes, homeowner's insurance, homeowner's association dues. *As the payment includes these things (other than principal), you will need to gather this information, too.

Per the guidelines, the lender's payment is determined as follows: Deduct interest, property taxes, homeowner's insurance, and homeowner's association dues from the 31% figure. The remaining balance is the MAXIMUM your 1st Mortgage Payment can be.

If your current payment prior to modification is already BELOW this figure, your modification under HAMP will not be approved.

STEP TWO:

HOW DOES THE LENDER GET YOU TO THAT MAXIMUM 1ST MORTGAGE PAYMENT?

1. Lowering your interest rate to as low as 2% start rate.

-or-

2. Extending the term of your mortgage to 40 years in order to lower the payment and get you to 31%.

Principal Forgiveness – Deferring Principal

*At the lender's discretion, they may defer some of your principal balance and not charge interest on a portion of the balance. Only a low percentage of lenders will do this, so do not have any expectations that it will happen. The forgiven amount is usually payable if you refinance, at the end of the term of the mortgage or when you sell.

If your maximum payment did not get to 31% of your gross income using the first two steps and your lender does not subscribe to deferring principal, then your HAMP request can possibly qualify for another internal program or be denied. If denied, then you need to increase your income. Try to lower your insurance and property taxes, if possible, and then reapply.

Let your lender know that you have new information to submit. Keep your time line in mind and don't forget to write down names, departments, and dates.

NOTE: The lender will verify your income, so if you just give them income information over the phone don't be tempted to not be truthful because in the end you need to back it up on paper. Also, after the 3-month trial they will re-verify the income to make sure it has not increased, etc.

CHAPTER THIRTEEN

NPV OVERVIEW
WHAT THE HECK IS NPV?

Most borrowers have no idea what an NPV calculator is and don't have a clue why they failed it. Here is the definition of NPV as it relates to the Home Affordable Modification Program (HAMP):

The Net Present Value ("NPV") is a formula used to determine your eligibility for a loan modification under the HAMP Program. The purpose in running an NPV calculation is to decide if the investor of your mortgage is in a better profit position by approving you for a modification (basically which choice gets them more money is the bottom line), or if they would have a higher profit margin by allowing a property to foreclose.

If the borrower is not approved for a HAMP modification because the transaction failed the NPV calculations, then the service must explain what the NPV means, tell you the factors used to make the NPV decision, and advise you that you may request the values used in making the calculations, along with the date the process was completed, within 30 days of the notice of denial. The reason they have to provide this information to you is to give you the opportunity to make any necessary corrections to the values they used, as they make or break your ability to be considered eligible under the HAMP program.

You or your authorized representative can request the specific NPV values verbally, or by writing to the servicer, within 30 calendar days from the notice date, and they must answer your request within 10 days.

If you request the NPV values and you have a foreclosure sale pending, the service must not complete the foreclosure sale until 30 days after they deliver those values to you to give you time to correct the inaccurate values, if there are any.

Once the evidence that the NPV values used were inaccurate, the servicer has the burden to make the necessary verifications to see if the corrections are material to the outcome of the NPV.

Some values don't affect the outcome and do not warrant a change from the NPV. If you find inaccurate values in the NPV calculations and you follow the protocol for advising the lender, your servicer must reconcile the inaccuracies prior to proceeding with any foreclosure sale.

As always, the best way to win at the loan modification game is to learn everything you can about the process so you can be empowered and successful with your loan modification and saving your home. Be prepared to question and challenge the lender and get the information that was used. You have right to obtain this information.

Work on finding opportunities to increase your income if it is too low to qualify or if you have been denied. The lender does not use your expenses or credit card debt in calculating these figures, but if you carry a large credit debt load, you will be referred to a credit-counseling agency. I would also suggest debt settlement if you are already late on you other bills, as well.

WHAT IS NET PRESENT VALUE OR NPV?

Here is the official NPV definition:

"NPV is the total present value of a time series of cash flows. It is a formula used to take each cash flow expected in the future and discount it back to its present value. Each present value is then added together and the sum (minus any outflow) is the net present value of the cash flows at the rate used to discount it back."

Confused? Essentially, NPV compares the value of a dollar today to the value of that same dollar in the future.

So what does this all mean?

Get Ready
NPV in Depth: New Guidelines

The HAMP NPV Guidelines were revised in February 2011.

Investors have instructed servicers to use NPV, and legislators have attempted to provide some assurance that use of an NPV test to justify modifications would be upheld if challenged (although these are really just declarations of legislative opinion and may not be binding on courts).

How do servicers apply this test?

The Answer Is...

First, a loan servicer should determine the net present value of the proceeds expected to be received from liquidation and sale of the mortgaged property for the loan under consideration, if the servicer were to foreclose on the loan, taking into account, based on reasonable estimates where applicable:

(i) the current market value as indicated by a broker's price opinion, automated valuation methodology, or appraisal;

(ii) the costs to foreclose, repair and maintain the mortgaged property;

(iii) the time to dispose of the mortgaged property if not sold to a third party bidder at the foreclosure sale;

(iv) the costs that will be incurred to market and sell the property as real estate owned; and

(v) the net sales proceeds. The discount rate to be used to calculate the net present value might be the net mortgage rate due to the investors.

The resulting number is the "Liquidation Proceeds NPV."

Next, the servicer should calculate the NPV of the cash flows expected from a loan modification that is successfully paid. This obviously assumes that the payment is affordable – we'll get to that in a bit. Then, everything else being equal, the servicer should select whichever results in the higher NPV. Sometimes, that solution will be to foreclose because, based on the calculations and some assumptions, the servicer has determined that it makes sense to liquidate and take the loss on foreclosing now. Other times, especially in a declining real estate market where the property's value has significantly deteriorated since the loan was originated, the NPV test will show that it may make better economic sense to modify the loan drastically and keep the borrower in the home and continue some cash flow.

NPV Reformed Rules for Consumers

On February 1, 2011, HAMP servicers will begin to implement the changes brought into existence by Section 1482(a) and (b) of the Dodd-Frank Act, also known as the Dodd-Frank Wall Street Reform and Consumer Protection Act.

This act will bring some much-needed reform to the current processing disaster being experienced by homeowners who are being denied due to NPV. The notices will be revised to now include the following:

• A list of borrower and mortgage-related Net Present Value (NPV) input fields and the values used in the NPV calculation to evaluate the borrower's first lien mortgage loan.

• Changes to the process by which borrowers request NPV inputs.

• Guidance relating to borrowers who dispute the property value used by the servicer for the "Property Value" input in the NPV calculation.

In addition, they are working on a borrower NPV calculator; they expect to be available by spring 2011.

For up-to-date information on NPV rules, visit:
www.theloanmodguru.com

Dodd-Frank Act NPV Notice Requirements

If you are not approved for a trial plan or permanent HAMP loan modification, you servicer (in the case of this announcement, not Freddie Mac or Fannie Mae backed mortgages) is required to send you a Non-Approval Notice, which explains the reason you are not approved and provides you with an opportunity to submit evidence that the information used in the evaluation was inaccurate. The servicer must also advise you if the NPV test was performed and whether the result of it was negative. This Non-Approval Notice must include the NPV input values, wherein previously you had to request them. They will also be required to send you the NPV Data Input Fields and Values chart.

The servicer will be required to provide information on how to communicate with them if you wish to dispute the reasons for the non-approval determination and where you can send your evidence and appeal in writing.

The purpose of providing you with the NPV values is to give you an opportunity to see what information was used to determine that you were ineligible due to a negative NPV and allow you to correct any of the information that impacted your eligibility. You have 30 days from the date of the Non-Approval Notice to submit the written evidence of any inaccuracies in your NPV inputs to the servicer; if you are disputing more than one input, provide documentation for each item within the same correspondence. Make sure it is faxed and delivered overnight with a return receipt request to avoid the other headaches you may have experienced in regards to lost documentation. The servicer cannot conduct a foreclosure sale until they review the inaccuracies, but follow up on your part is highly suggested.

If the information you provide is valid and can make a change to the NPV outcome, then the servicer must perform the NPV calculation with the corrected information, and the servicer must provide the updated outcome and newly input values to you, the borrower.

You may also be directed to seek assistance directly from MHA or HOPE prior to contacting the servicer, and they can do a preliminary run of your corrected inputs. However, if by using your updated information your results are still negative, then you are not eligible for another re-evaluation or appeal for other inputs by either MHA, HOPE, or the Servicer.

This goes on to be a bit vague because it says you can still go to them for help in WRITING ONLY for the remainder of the 30 days, but it states that they will not accept an appeal for any "other" inputs.

DISPUTED PROPERTY VALUE INPUT

For the first time ever, they are speaking to another huge issue that borrowers have faced—the issue of the incorrect property value being used and the servicer's refusal to give homeowners the property value they used to deny you for negative NPV. So, if you are not approved for HAMP because of negative NPV and you believe the property value they are using differs from the fair market value of the property as of the initial date they ran the NPV, then you may request an NPV re-evaluation within 30 days of the Non-Approval Notice. You must provide an estimate of the property value, along with any other documentation of any other material disputed inputs.

If the preliminary re-evaluation using this information results in a positive NPV result, then you have 15 calendar days from the date of the notification that the preliminary NPV result is positive to submit a $200 deposit against the full cost of the appraisal by a licensed appraiser not affiliated with the servicer. The servicer will add the balance of the actual appraisal cost to your total arrearages. However, the servicer will not be required to obtain a new appraisal if they had already obtained one performed in accordance with the standards listed here. They must provide you with a copy of the appraisal. *See NPV Letter in the Reference Guide.

On the following page is a chart that shows an example of a calculation to compare the Liquidation Proceeds NPV and the NPV of a loan modification.

SAVE YOUR HOME ● NPV OVERVIEW

UPB Reduction / Deferral:		20%	

	Scenario		
	As Is	Modification	Loan Default Liquidation
UPB	$483,339.66	$386,671.73	$483,339.66
Interest Rate	9.4%	9.4%	9.4%
Term	340	340	340
Monthly Payment	$4,073.08	$3,258.46 *	$4,073.08
Market Value	$507,506.64	$507,506.64 *	$507,506.64
Discount Rate	9.4%	9.4%	9.4%
NPV	$483,339.66	$393,481.28	$253,596.46

Variables which can be Modified

Difference in NPV between mod & liquidation $139,884.81

Month	Investor Cash Flow	Investor Cash Flow	Investor Cash Flow	
20	$4,073.08	$3,258.46	$4,073.08	Default in month 20
21	$4,073.08	$3,258.46	$4,073.08	Difference in monthly
22	$4,073.08	$3,258.46	$4,073.08	payment
23	$4,073.08	$3,258.46	$4,073.08	(Scheduled P&I
24	$4,073.08	$3,258.46	$4,073.08	advanced to investor)
25	$4,073.08	$3,258.46	$4,073.08	
26	$4,073.08	$3,258.46	$4,073.08	
27	$4,073.08	$3,258.46	$4,073.08	
28	$4,073.08	$3,258.46	$4,073.08	
29	$4,073.08	$3,258.46	$4,073.08	
30	$4,073.08	$3,258.46	$4,073.08	
31	$4,073.08	$3,258.46	$4,073.08	
32	$4,073.08	$3,258.46	$4,073.08	
33	$4,073.08	$3,258.46	$4,073.08	
34	$4,073.08	$3,258.46	$4,073.08	
35	$4,073.08	$3,258.46	$4,073.08	
36	$4,073.08	$3,258.46	$4,073.08	Net sale proceeds at REO sale after paying the
37	$4,073.08	$3,258.46	$217,502.85	servicer back its advances, and after
38	$4,073.08	$3,258.46		maintenance, taxes and marketing, brokerage
39	$4,073.08	$3,258.46		and other costs in connection with the sale
40	$4,073.08	$3,258.46		
:				
:				Liquidated loan, no more
:				payments
:				
360	$4,073.08	$3,258.46		
Balloon (20% UPB):	$0.00	$96,667.93		

Difference in monthly payment ($814.62)

* This payment is based on amortization of the reduced UPB at the note rate; balloon does not accrue interest.

119

SECTION SEVEN

IF YOU'RE NOT LATE ON YOUR MORTGAGE

CHAPTER FOURTEEN

HAMP GUIDELINE

Reasonably Foreseeable
(Imminent) Default

A borrower that is current or less than 60 days delinquent who contacts the servicer for a modification, appears potentially eligible for a modification, and claims a hardship must under Supplemental Directive 09-01 Page 3 be screened for imminent default. The servicer must make a determination as to whether a payment default is imminent, based on the servicer's standards for imminent default and consistent with applicable contractual agreements and accounting standards. If the servicer determines that default is imminent, the servicer must apply the Net Present Value test. In the process of making its imminent default determination, the servicer must evaluate the borrower's financial condition in light of the borrower's hardship, as well as inquire as to the condition of and circumstances affecting the property securing the mortgage loan. The servicer must consider the borrower's financial condition, liquid assets, liabilities, combined monthly income from wages and all other identified sources of income, monthly obligations (including personal debts, revolving accounts, and installment loans), and a reasonable allowance for living expenses such as food, utilities, etc. The hardship and financial condition of the borrower shall be verified through documentation. In documenting the Reason for and Timing of Imminent Default, a servicer must document in its servicing system the basis for its determination that a payment default is imminent and retain all documentation used to reach its conclusion. The servicer's documentation must also include information on the borrower's financial condition, as well as the condition and circumstances of the property securing the mortgage loan.

To be considered as qualifying for HAMP Home Affordable Modification Program, even when you are NOT currently delinquent, this formula must be used by your servicer, and the borrower's debt coverage ratio must be less than 1.20. This is sometimes difficult to figure out, so I have explained the step-by-step process.

This is how the lender calculates this formula to see if your account is in "imminent" danger of becoming delinquent, in other words, to figure out if you seem like you may become delinquent very soon.

A. To come up with what they call Debt Coverage Ratio, you first take your net or your after-tax and deduction income, minus escrow amounts (monthly property tax, homeowners insurance, Homeowner Association fees), also minus all other credit obligations (any obligations on your credit, such as credit cards, loans, auto payments, etc), minus living expenses (such as utilities, gas, auto insurance, food etc.), minus negative rental income or investment property mortgages.

Once you come up with this figure, divide the figure by the figure you get from the calculation below.

B. Now take the current first mortgage payment, including principal and interest, but NOT counting escrow or taxes and insurance.

A divided by B = Debt Coverage Ratio

The number you get is called the debt coverage ratio. This is the exact calculation your servicer will use to verify you have a hardship and whether you may be facing foreclosure when you are NOT behind in your mortgage payments to see if you can apply for the HAMP Home Affordable Modification Program per the exact guidelines your participating servicer must follow per the Treasury Department, Fannie Mae, and Freddie Mac as of 1/01/2010.

If you get less than 1.20, you can be considered at risk for defaulting on your payment AND you must also have less than three monthly total current mortgage payments, including property tax and homeowners insurance payments, in liquid assets cash reserves that you have available from any financial or brokerage institution, such as checking, savings, certificate of deposits, mutual funds, stocks, bonds or money market accounts (even if they are held for an extended term).

If you pass both of these tests, you get a ratio of less than 1.20, AND you have less than the three months in liquid reserves, then this signals the servicer to proceed and begin the process of eligibility for the HAMP Loan Modification Program.

Do the calculations above to see where you stand.

IF the figure you get here is over 1.20, then you will not be considered as being in danger of facing a financial hardship and you will not be considered for the HAMP

President Obama Program when you have not missed a mortgage payment.

CHAPTER FIFTEEN

THE FORECLOSURE TIMELINE

Source:
http://resources.lawinfo.com/en/Articles/Consumer-Finance-and-Foreclosure/Federal/the-foreclosure-timeline.html

Though the foreclosure timeline varies by state, the U.S. Housing and Urban Development Department offers the following timeline of events involved in losing your home:

First month missed payment – your lender will contact you by letter or phone. A housing counselor can help.

Second month missed payment – your lender is likely to begin calling you to discuss why you have not made your payments. It is important that you take their phone calls. Talk to your lender and explain your situation and what you are trying to do to resolve it. At this time, you still may be able to make one payment to prevent yourself from falling three months behind. A housing counselor can help.

Third month missed payment – after the third payment is missed, you will receive a letter from your lender stating the amount you are delinquent, and that you have 30 days to bring your mortgage current. This is called a "Demand Letter" or "Notice to Accelerate." If you do not pay the specified amount or make some type of arrangements by the given date, the lender may begin foreclosure proceedings. They are unlikely to accept less than the total due without arrangements being made if you receive this letter. You still have time to work something out with your lender. A housing counselor can still help.

Fourth month missed payment – now you are nearing the end of time allowed in your Demand or Notice to Accelerate Letter. When the 30 days ends, if you have not paid the full amount or worked out arrangements, you will be referred to your lender's attorneys. You will incur all attorney fees as part of your delinquency. A housing counselor can still help you.

Sheriff's or Public Trustee's Sale – the attorney will schedule a Sale. This is the actual day of foreclosure. You may be notified of the date by mail, a notice is taped to your door, and the sale may be advertised in a local paper. The time between the Demand or Notice to Accelerate Letter and the actual Sale varies by state. In some states, it can be as quick as 2 to 3 months. This is not the move-out date, but the end is near. You have until the date of sale to make arrangements with your lender, or pay the total amount owed, including attorney fees.

Redemption Period – after the sale date, you may enter a redemption period. You will be notified of your time frame on the same notice that your state uses for your Sheriff's or Public Trustee's Sale.

FORECLOSURE LAWS BY STATE

Page source:
http://www.realtytrac.com/foreclosure-laws/foreclosure-laws-comparison.asp

State	Judicial	Non-Judicial	Comments	Process Period (Days)	Sale Publication (Days)	Redemption Period (Days)	Sale/NTS
Alabama	•	•	○	49-74	21	365	Trustee
Alaska	•	•	○	105	65	365*	Trustee
Arizona	•	•	○	90+	41	30-180*	Trustee
Arkansas	•	•	○	70	30	365*	Trustee
California	•	•	○	117	21	365*	Trustee
Colorado	•	•	○	145	60	None	Trustee
Connecticut	•		○	62	NA	Court Decides	Court
Delaware	•		○	170-210	60-90	None	Sheriff
District of Columbia		•	○	47	18	None	Trustee
Florida	•		○	135	NA	None	Court
Georgia	•	•	○	37	32	None	Trustee
Hawaii	•	•	○	220	60	None	Trustee
Idaho	•	•	○	150	45	365	Trustee
Illinois	•		○	300	NA	90	Court
Indiana	•		○	261	120	None	Sheriff
Iowa	•	•	○	160	30	20	Sheriff
Kansas	•		○	130	21	365	Sheriff
Kentucky	•		○	147	NA	365	Court
Louisiana	•		○	180	NA	None	Sheriff
Maine	•		○	240	30	90	Court
Maryland	•		○	46	30	Court Decides	Court
Massachusetts	•		○	75	41	None	Court
Michigan		•	○	60	30	30-365	Sheriff
Minnesota	•	•	○	90-100	7	1825	Sheriff
Mississippi	•	•	○	90	30	None	Trustee
Missouri	•	•	○	60	10	365	Trustee
Montana	•	•	○	150	50	None	Trustee
Nebraska	•		○	142	NA	None	Sheriff

State	Judicial	Non-Judicial	Comments	Process Period (Days)	Sale Publication (Days)	Redemption Period (Days)	Sale/NTS
Nevada	•	•	◔	116	80	None	Trustee
New Hampshire		•	◔	59	24	None	Trustee
New Jersey	•		◔	270	NA	10	Sheriff
New Mexico	•		◔	180	NA	30-270	Court
New York	•		◔	445	NA	None	Court
North Carolina	•	•	◔	110	25	None	Sheriff
North Dakota	•		◔	150	NA	180-365	Sheriff
Ohio	•		◔	217	NA	None	Sheriff
Oklahoma	•	•	◔	186	NA	None	Sheriff
Oregon	•	•	◔	150	30	180	Trustee
Pennsylvania	•		◔	270	NA	None	Sheriff
Rhode Island	•	•	◔	62	21	None	Trustee
South Carolina	•		◔	150	NA	None	Court
South Dakota	•	•	◔	150	23	30-365	Sheriff
Tennessee		•	◔	40-45	20-25	730	Trustee
Texas	•	•	◔	27	NA	None	Trustee
Utah			◔	142	NA	Court Decides	Trustee
Vermont	•		◔	95	NA	180-365	Court
Virginia	•	•	◔	45	14-28	None	Trustee
Washington	•	•	◔	135	90	None	Trustee
West Virginia		•	◔	60-90	30-60	None	Trustee
Wisconsin	•	•	◔	290	NA	365	Sheriff
Wyoming	•	•	◔	60	25	90-365	Sheriff

* Judicial Only   Mouseover the ◔ symbol to view state-specific comments

CHAPTER SIXTEEN

THE CASE OF THE MISSING OR INCOMPLETE DOCUMENTS

L ately, there has been a surge of denials for incomplete information, either because they did not acknowledge receipt of the documents, or they say they never received them or gave you too little time to provide the updated documents. In the Reference Section, I've included a letter you can use if you have been denied after being given limited time to provide the requested documents (Sample Letter #1). With the issue of documents not being received, I suggest calling every day to check if they received your fax and having them note your account that you sent them. Verify, Verify, Verify! When possible, request an email address to email the documents directly. Mail in a copy of the documents (get return receipts), and save all fax confirmations. Verify receipt of everything you send. (See Sample Letter #1 in the Reference Section)

Get the documents you need and a Comprehensive Do It Yourself System Available at www.theloanmodguru.com

CHAPTER SEVENTEEN

NOTICE OF NON-APPROVAL

F or borrowers not approved for a HAMP modification, this notice must provide the primary reason or reasons for the non-approval. The notice must also describe other foreclosure prevention alternatives for which the borrower may be eligible, if any, including, but not limited to: other modification programs, pre-foreclosure sale, or deed-in-lieu of foreclosure. The notice must identify the steps the borrower must take in order to be considered for those alternatives. If the servicer has already approved the borrower for another foreclosure prevention alternative, information necessary to participate in or complete the alternative should be included. The notice should be clear that the borrower was considered, but is not eligible for HAMP.

If you have been denied for a HAMP modification, find out exactly why and reapply. If your numbers have changed, you can reapply immediately. It is of utmost importance for you to remain calm and find out in great detail all of the reasons for being declined. Many people who have received a denial can get approved for loan modification if they have changes to their previously submitted information and submit them. Being denied is frustrating and scary, but it definitely does not mean it is the only chance you have. If you are determined to keep your home and you know you can make a reasonable payment, you still have a chance to make it work. Don't be discouraged. I know there are people who have been denied up to 10 times for loan modifications that end up saving their homes because of their determination and refusal to give up, even when it seemed they had no hope.

Common reasons for denial are:

◇ Insufficient income

◇ Too much income

◇ Current payment is already below 31% of your gross income

◇ Too much money in the bank

◇ Borrower is not living in the property

◇ Lack of hardship

◇ Voluntarily left job

◇ Went back to school

◇ Lender could not reach borrower

◇ Incomplete application/missing information

◇ Lender feels that default is likely to happen with the information submitted

◇ Borrower did not make trial payments on time as required for permanent modification

◇ Income changes were more than 25% different than when borrower originally qualified

◇ No imminent default

*See page 124.

We are all human, and in my experience, I have witnessed **many** make a mistake in these areas.

Negotiators at many of the lenders have told me that the lack of explanation of the hardship is another big reason people are being denied. Consider all of these factors when writing your Hardship Letter. Make sure you include all of the reasons you have a hardship, and that you are in need of help. Try to keep it to one page, if possible, and be articulate and to the point.

Affirmation:

I can choose to focus on the positive in every situation.

CHAPTER EIGHTEEN

IF YOU GET STUCK

There is honest help available!

DON'T GIVE UP! Don't listen to people who mean well but don't know what they are talking about; i.e., neighbors, friends, and strangers. Only seek advice from knowledgeable people you can really trust. Don't pay anyone who comes knocking on your door or calls you on the phone.

You will find that if you follow the steps in this book closely, especially the mindset and organization, along with your perseverance, you most likely will not need help. In the event you do, there is honest help available.

If you get stuck and need help, contact agencies such as the HOPE Hotline, 1-888-995-4673 (HOPE), available 24 hours a day, 7 days a week, in English and Spanish. You will already be way ahead of the game, as you will be organized, with your package and information ready. You will have full knowledge of your situation and be able to explain things clearly so that you can work as a team to save your home. The same rules apply here; you must be responsible in the communication and follow up of your case file. As another option, you can contact HUD (800-569-4287) for a list of attorneys that specialize in these situations, or to schedule a face-to-face appointment with your lender (in states where applicable). For additional assistance, you can contact NACA: 888-302-NACA www.NACA.com.

Advice: For best results, be completely prepared and organized with all of your income, expenses, and documents as explained in the previous chapters of this book.

Steps to Prevent Foreclosure

Foreclosure Prevention Steps

If you're at a place where you know you can't make your mortgage payment, then you need to address the problem. Ignoring it will not make it go away. In fact, it will make it worse.

If your lender has contacted you about your late mortgage payment, here are some things you can do to prevent foreclosure.

1. Address the problem immediately.

As soon as you are aware that you can't make your payment, address the problem. Begin finding ways to either come up with the money you need to make the payment, catch up on your late payments or prepare to apply for a loan modification.

2. Take the initiative and immediately talk to your lender.

The bank doesn't *really* want your house. They want your money. They also want your payments to be current—it makes their job easier. Get prepared with all of your accurate financial information first, then contact them. Be forthright and tell them what your situation is and what you can do to resolve matters and bring your payments up to date. Ask them what they are willing to do or can do to help you through this situation. Above all, let them know that you are sincere and want to work with them to prevent foreclosure.

3. Read any and all mail you receive from lenders.

Ignoring it or putting it off will only make matters worse. Read every correspondence you receive from the bank. Initially, they'll give you a "friendly" notice, often providing you with homeowner's counseling information that can be of good use to you. As time goes on, though, the notices will become more demanding and might inform you of their intention to take legal action. The sooner you know and act on this information, the better. In court, they don't have to prove that you read their correspondence—just that they sent it to you. Keep the dates on a calendar and DO NOT miss any deadlines.

4. Become informed about your rights and options.

The information in this book is a good start. Take time also to read all of your mortgage loan documents and find out what steps your lender your lender will take in the event you cannot make your payments as scheduled. Being informed is one of the best ways to be prepared. Find out about what loan modification programs are available and find out what the guidelines are and see where you fit in.

5. Find out what options you have to prevent foreclosure.

What options will your lender provide? What options does the government provide? Go to reliable sources on the Internet, such as government Making Home Affordable, FHA or VA and your bank's websites, to learn what you can do to save your home.

6. Get housing counseling.

Make an appointment with a housing counselor, who will advise you about the law and any options you may have. This counselor is also skilled in reviewing your finances and can help you create a budget and spending plan that might make it easier for you to make your payments. Some housing counselors can also act as your representative with your lender. However, do not let a housing counselor act on your behalf without knowing everything that is occurring in any negotiations. Housing counselors are great advocates, but you must become your own best advocate first, they can only help you with the information you give them, so be as prepared as possible so you can use this valuable ally, and begin thinking of alternatives in raising your income and/or lowering your debt if necessary.

> **More lenders are employing housing counselors of their own if that bank has a local branch where they might be able to speak with a housing counselor from their lender.**

7. Find the money you need to make your payments.

If you can't make your monthly payment, take a long hard look at your finances. Cut anything and everything that is not a necessity. This could mean cell phones, cable or satellite TV, memberships, eating out, or your $5 morning cup of coffee. Are there any bills you can put off paying until you're caught up, such as credit card bills? Wouldn't you rather default on a credit card than lose your home? Once you've found additional funds in that way, look for ways you can get additional income. Sell a car, jewelry, or a pool table. Tap into your 401K or a life insurance policy, if you can. Get an extra job, even if it's babysitting for someone's children on the weekends. This will bring in some additional income and show the bank that you are sincere and are taking active measures to make your payments.

8. Be aware of scams.

Unfortunately, there are foreclosure recovery companies that take advantage of homeowners when they are in need. Don't fall prey to them. Never sign any legal document or transfer any ownership in your home without knowing what you're signing and getting it reviewed by an attorney, a licensed and trusted realtor, or credit counselor. While you may think you're hiring them to prevent foreclosure, you might, in fact, be signing your house over to them.

Affirmation:

*I appreciate all the blessings in my life
and am grateful daily.*

CHAPTER NINETEEN

OVERTURNING A FORECLOSURE SALE

O verturning a foreclosure trustee sale is an extremely difficult task to take on, but in some cases, if the conditions are just right and your determination is unfailing, it can and has been done.

I have personally overturned 14 foreclosure sales, but let me tell you that each and every single one of them was more than a full-time job. My life in general became only about overturning the sale; someone's home was at stake and for me that was the motivating factor that made me relentless. Every second had to be devoted to writing emails and letters to every person I could think of that might be able to help overturn the sale. From government officials to bank executives, everyone must be contacted and involved. Not everyone is willing to put the rest of his or her life on hold and undertake this sort of painstaking and strenuous venture, so be prepared.

You have been warned.

Before you undertake this task, you must be completely sure that you should have qualified for a loan modification, and in all of the cases I took on to advocate, there was some sort of provable bank error.

So here are the keys to making this happen:

- Know your financials perfectly

- Have your facts straight

- Keep your timelines and conversations documented

- Have your paper trail in order

- Research all of the guidelines you feel were not followed and be ready to cite them sparingly

- Reach out to every key person you can via email, overnight letters, and faxes, and I mean everybody.

The step-by-step procedure to accomplish this is too involved to include in this book. However, every skill contained here, along with the keys listed above, proved instrumental. To succeed at overturning a foreclosure sale, everything was followed to the letter, and these keys can be used for postponing a sale, too.

CHAPTER TWENTY

OTHER OPTIONS THAT SHOULD ONLY BE YOUR LAST RESORT

I f you have truly exhausted all modification options, here are some other options that you can consider. In some cases, they will provide you with a temporary means of stopping foreclosure. In others, you will need to leave your home and seek a fresh start. Please consult with a professional before deciding on any of these options.

Many people have been approved after multiple denials.

Advice: Know what is wrong and find solutions, i.e., more income or corrections to expenses.

- Bankruptcy (may stop the foreclosure sale)
- Short payoff
- Deed-in-lieu
- Postponement of sale
- Walk away plan
- Rate, term and/or principal reduction
- Repayment plan
- Forbearance
- Reinstatement
- Foreclosure
- Short sale

CHAPTER TWENTY-ONE

MILITARY HOMEOWNERS HAVE PROTECTION AGAINST FORECLOSURE: BE AWARE

T here are several lenders offering special programs for our eligible service members. Bank of America offers special assistance programs for servicemen and woman and there are many other benefits available to you under the under the Servicemembers Civil Relief Act (also known as the SCRA) I have included the HUD explanation for (loan) servicers.

Who Is Eligible?

The provisions of the SCRA apply to active duty military personnel - members of the Army, Navy, Marine Corps, Air Force, Coast Guard; commissioned officers of the Public Health Service and the National Oceanic and Atmospheric Administration who are engaged in active service; reservists ordered to report for military service; persons ordered to report for induction under the Military Selective Service Act; guardsmen called to active service for more than 30 consecutive days - who had a mortgage obligation prior to enlistment or induction for an initial tour of duty or prior to recall after a break in service when subsequently ordered to active duty. In limited situations, dependents of servicemembers are also entitled to protections.

Is the Homeowner Protected Against Foreclosure?

Mortgage lenders may not foreclose, or seize property for a failure to pay a mortgage debt, while a service member is on active duty for 9 months grace period prior to December 31, 2012 unless they have the approval of a court. After December 31, 2012, the grace period for Service member's protection will revert back to 3 months. In a court proceeding, the lender would be required to show that the service member's ability to repay the debt was not affected by his or her military service.

Is This Relief Only Available for Borrowers with FHA-insured Mortgages?

No, the provisions of the SCRA apply to both conventional and government-insured mortgages.

How Many Reservists and Guardsmen Will Get This Relief?

HUD does not have data on the number of reservists and guardsmen that have mortgages eligible for interest rate reduction to six percent and other SCRA relief.

Who Pays for This Relief?

It depends on how the mortgage was financed. In recent years, the majority of FHA-insured mortgages have been financed using Ginnie Mae mortgage-backed securities or state government issued bonds.

If the mortgage is in a Ginnie Mae pool, Ginnie Mae will reimburse the issuer for interest in excess of six percent for payments that are collected on eligible loans. Other security issuers and government bond issuers may have different policies. Mortgagees should seek advice from

142

their legal counsel. Since the maximum allowable interest is six percent, a document other than the mortgage or note will be the determining factor.

HUD regulations authorize mortgagees to postpone or suspend foreclosure proceedings on FHA-insured mortgages to borrowers in active duty military service as defined in the SCRA. Under 24 CFR 203.346, the period during which the mortgagor is in military service shall be excluded in computing the period during which the mortgagee shall commence foreclosure or acquire the property by other means. Further, postponement or delay in prosecuting foreclosure proceedings during the period the mortgagor is in military service shall not be construed as a failure to exercise reasonable diligence. Thus, the mortgagee should not experience an interest curtailment due to foreclosure delay if an insurance claim is eventually filed with the Department. The reimbursed interest would be at the debenture rate.

How Much Will the Relief Cost the Housing Industry?

The costs of the relief cannot be estimated because there are unknown factors - for example, the number of active duty servicemembers who will seek mortgage relief.

What Should Reservists and Guardsmen Do to Take Advantage of the Act?

Reservists, guardsmen and other eligible servicemembers should contact their lenders and other creditors and provide documentation that they have been called to active duty and, therefore, are eligible for certain relief under the SCRA. Lenders should already be aware of the SCRA and its relief provisions.

143

Does the Act Apply to All Those on Active Duty?

Yes, all personnel on active military duty are eligible for the reduced interest rates on debts that were incurred prior to enlistment in the military, or prior to the activation of a reservist or guardsman, unless in the opinion of the court, the ability to pay is not materially affected by reason of such service.

Does This Apply to Reservists and Guardsmen in the Process of Buying Homes?

No. The SCRA applies if the closing on the house occurs prior to the reservist or guardsman being ordered to active duty.

Are There Any Mortgage Considerations in the Event that an Eligible Servicemember Is Killed?

The Act does not address this matter. For FHA-insured loans, however, you are required to work with the surviving family members to consider all applicable loss mitigation options to save the family home through a special forbearance plan, loan modification or partial claim, or avoid foreclosure through a Pre-foreclosure sale or deed-in-lieu of foreclosure.

Reprinted with permission from government HUD website:

http://portal.hud.gov:80/hudportal/HUD?src=/program_offices/housing/sfh/nsc/qasscra2

SECTION EIGHT

SAVE YOUR HOME RESOURCES

CHAPTER TWENTY-TWO

OTHER CONSIDERATIONS

WAYS TO INCREASE YOUR INCOME

I f your lender tells you that you do not have sufficient income for modification, consider these ways to increase it:

- Include income from other household members, Even if they are not on the loan
- If any family member contributes to paying anything for you, including debts, get proof and a letter of explanation
- Turn a skill into a side job
- Rent a room or two in your house to someone
- Ask for a raise
- Get a part-time second job

WAYS TO DECREASE YOUR EXPENSES

You should also think of ways to decrease your living expenses to keep your home:

- Check your home's value and lower your property taxes
- Check your homeowner's insurance policy to make sure you don't have forced placed insurance from the lender, or shop around for a

lower policy; if necessary, increase your deductible.

- Compare and shop around for your auto insurance
- Check your cell phone plan and find the best rate
- Clip coupons
- Turn lights off
- Trade in your car for one with lower payments, or if you have not made your mortgage payments, maybe you can get a cheaper car for cash
- Analyze your credit cards. Call your credit companies and try to lower the interest rates and payments or pay some debt off, if possible, to put yourself in a better position
- Drink water
- Cut back on spending
- Reduce unnecessary expenses

CHAPTER TWENTY-THREE

PREPARING YOUR PROFIT AND LOSS STATEMENT IF YOU ARE SELF EMPLOYED

(Make sure you get tax advice from a CPA)

T ypically, if you are self-employed or receive 1099 income, then you need a two-year track record. Lenders go by what you declare to the IRS as income, since that is documented. As some self-employed people overstate their expenses, this may then understate your income. Look at the schedule C of your tax returns for the last two years and the number at the bottom that says "profit" as your annual income. You can add any depreciation to that figure. Add them together and divide by twenty-four.

For modification purposes, you will use a Profit and Loss form that you can request from your CPA or you can create one yourself. Be careful with too many write-offs that leave you with no income, as the lender will take the bottom line profit number. If you write everything off, this number is sometimes not accurate. The lender is not in the business of reporting your income to the IRS, so be truthful about what you bring in when applying for your modification. Also, if you list an expense, such as an auto payment under the business, make sure you don't include it with your debt on the financial worksheet. If necessary, write a letter of explanation.

Here is an example of a possible Profit and Loss worksheet that you could submit along with your modification application:

Profit and Loss Statement
<Company Name>

For the <Month or Year> ending <Month-Day-Year> **Stated in 000s**

Gross margin [L/J] -
Return on sales [T/J] -

	Prior Period	Budget	Current Period	Current Period as % of Sales	% Change from Prior Period	% Change from Budget
Sales Revenue						
Product/Service 1				-	-	-
Product/Service 2				-	-	-
Product/Service 3				-	-	-
Product/Service 4				-	-	-
Total Sales Revenue [J]	0	0	0	-	-	-
Cost of Sales						
Product/Service 1				-	-	-
Product/Service 2				-	-	-
Product/Service 3				-	-	-
Product/Service 4				-	-	-
Total Cost of Sales [K]	0	0	0	-	-	-
Gross Profit [L=J-K]	0	0	0	-	-	-
Operating Expenses						
Sales and Marketing						
Advertising				-	-	-
Direct marketing				-	-	-
Other expenses (specify)				-	-	-
Other expenses (specify)				-	-	-
Total Sales and Marketing	0	0	0	-	-	-

149

Expenses [M]

Research and Development

Technology licenses				-	-	-
Patents				-	-	-
Other expenses (specify)				-	-	-
Other expenses (specify)				-	-	-
Total Research and Development Expenses [N]	0	0	0	-	-	-

General and Administrative

Wages and salaries				-	-	-
Outside services				-	-	-
Supplies				-	-	-
Meals and entertainment				-	-	-
Rent				-	-	-
Telephone				-	-	-
Utilities				-	-	-
Depreciation				-	-	-
Insurance				-	-	-
Repairs and maintenance				-	-	-
Other expenses (specify)				-	-	-
Other expenses (specify)				-	-	-
Total General and Administrative Expenses [O]	0	0	0	-	-	-
Total Operating Expenses [P=M+N+O]	0	0	0	-	-	-
Income from Operations [Q=L-P]	0	0	0	-	-	-
Other Income [R]				-	-	-

Taxes

Income taxes				-	-	-
Payroll taxes				-	-	-
Real estate taxes				-	-	-
Other taxes (specify)				-	-	-
Other taxes (specify)				-	-	-
Total Taxes [S]	0	0	0	-	-	-
Net Profit [T=Q+R-S]	0	0	0	-	-	-

Contact your CPA for advice on Profit and Loss

SECTION NINE

SAVE YOUR HOME REFERENCE GUIDE

LENDER CONTACT LIST

ACQURA LOAN SERVICES
866.660.5804
http://www.acqura.net/

AMERICAN HOME MORTGAGE SERVICING (FORMERLY OPTION ONE MORTGAGE CORPORATION)
Call with mortgage questions: 1-800-505-3706
Home Preservation Number: 877-304.3100
Option One Customers: 888-275-2648
https://ahmsi3.com/servicing/home.asp
https://online.ahmsi3.com/servicing/BAT_bateam.asp

AMERICA'S SERVICING COMPANY (ASC)
https://carenet.fnfismd.com/wellsasc/

AMTRUST BANK
Call with mortgage questions: 888-696-4444
Home Preservation Number: 800-860-2025 ext.2897
http://www.amtrust.com/Personal/Mortgages/Pages/home.aspx
https://www.amtrust.com/Personal/Mortgages/Pages/MortgagePaymentAssistance.aspx

AURORA LOAN SERVICES
Call with mortgage questions: 800-550-0508
Home Preservation Number: 866-521-3828
http://www.myauroraloan.com/

BANK OF AMERICA
Call with mortgage questions: 1-800-846-2222
Home Preservation Number: 800-285-6000

http://www.bankofamerica.com/loansandhomes/financial-difficulty/
http://homeloans.bankofamerica.com/en/service-and-support/homeowner-relief/find-a-solution.html

BANK UNITED
877-779-2265
http://www.bankunited.com

CARRINGTON MORTGAGE SERVICES
Call with mortgage questions: 1-800-561-4567
800-790-9502
http://myloan.carringtonms.com

CENLAR MORTGAGE
800-223-6527
http://www.cenlar.com/

CENTRAL MORTGAGE COMPANY
800-366-2132
http://www.centralmortgageonline.com/

CCO MORTGAGE
866-612-6206
http://www.ccomortgage.com/

CHASE
Call with mortgage questions: 1-866-326-0086
Home Preservation Number: 866-345-4676
Prime 800-446-8939
Nonprime 877-838-1882
http://mortgage.chase.com/pages/shared/gateway.jsp
https://www.chase.com/chf/mortgage/keeping-your-home

CHEVY CHASE BANK, F.S.B.
http://www.chevychasebank.com/

CITI MORTGAGE (CITIMORTGAGE, CITIRESIDENTIAL, CITIFINANCIAL)

Call with mortgage questions: 1-866-915-9417
Home Preservation Number: 800-926-9783
800-695-0384
http://www.citimortgage.com/Mortgage/Home.do?page=hardship_assistance

COUNTRYWIDE HOME LOANS - NOW BANK OF AMERICA

(see Bank of America contacts above)
Call with mortgage questions: 1-800-669-6607
http://homeloans.bankofamerica.com/en/service-and-support/homeowner-relief/find-a-solution.html
http://my.countrywide.com/media/FinancialAssistance.html

EMC MORTGAGE CORPORATION

Home Preservation Number: 877-362-6631
https://www.emcmortgagecorp.com/EMCMORTGAGE
http://www.emcmortgageservicing.com/
https://emcmortgagecorp.com/emcccn/faq/keepmyhome.jsp

EVERHOME MORTGAGE

Call with mortgage questions: 800-669-9721
Home Preservation Number: 800-669-7724
http://www.everhomemortgage.com/
http://www.everhomemortgage.com/502PaymentTroubles.asp

5/3 FIFTH THIRD BANK

Call with mortgage questions: 1-800-375-1745 dial option 3

https://www.53.com/wps/portal/content/?New_WCM_
Context=/wps/wcm/connect/BetterTomorrow/BetterTo
morrow+Landing/Mortgage/

FIRST FRANKLIN LOAN SERVICES
Call with mortgage questions: 1-800-346-6437
www.viewmyloan.com

FIRST HORIZON
800-364-7662
http://www.firsthorizon.com/

FLAGSTAR BANK
Home Preservation Number: 800-968-7700
https://www.flagstar.com/personal/home-
loans/mortgagepaymentrelief.html

**GMAC RESCAP – GMAC MORTGAGE,
HOMECOMINGS FINANCIAL, GMAC BANK AND
DITECH**
Call with mortgage questions: 1-800-206-2901 or call
586-443-4450
Home Preservation Number: 800-766-4642
http://www.homecomings.com
http://www.gmacmortgage.com
http://www.ditech.com
http://www.gmacmortgage.com/Resource_Center/home
owner_help/homeowner_help.html

GREENPOINT MORTGAGE FUNDING
http://www.greenpointservice.com/

HOMEQ SERVICING
Call with mortgage questions: 1-888-320-6663
877-867-7378
http://www.homeq.com/
http://www.homeq.com/challenges/index.jsp

HSBC NORTH AMERICA – HFC AND BENEFICIAL
1-800-333-5848 (HFC and Beneficial customers)
1-800-365-6730 (HSBC Mortgage Services customers)
http://www.us.hsbc.com/1/2/3/personal/home-loans/mortgage/custservices
https://www.hsbcmortgageservices.com/managing_hardship_text
http://www.beneficial.com/

HUNTINGTON MORTGAGE GROUP
Call with mortgage questions: 1-800-323-9865
www.huntington.com

INDEPENDENT BANK
Call with mortgage questions: 1-800-292-5020
www.independentbank.com

INDYMAC BANK/ONEWEST BANK
Call with mortgage questions: 800-781-7399
Home Preservation Number: 877-908-4357
800-880-6848
www.imb.com
http://www.owb.com/singlecontent.aspx?id=1372

JP MORGAN CHASE / DEFAULT HPO HELP LINE
866-345-4676

LAND AMERICA LENDER SERVICES
800-909-9525
800-274-6600
email to: customersupport@myloancare.com

LITTON LOAN SERVICING / AVELO MORTGAGE L.L.C.
Call with mortgage questions: 1-866-416-1656
800-999-8501
https://www.littonloan.com/

https://www.littonloan.com/fin_info1.asp

LOANCARE SERVICING CENTER
Home Preservation Number: 800-909-9525
800-274-6600
http://www.myloancare.com/
M & T MORTGAGE CORPORATION
800-724-2224
https://www.mtb.com/personal/checking/Pages/mortga
gediscountoffer.aspx

NATIONAL CITY MORTGAGE
Call with mortgage questions: 1-800-367-9305 ext 58120
Home Preservation Number: 800-523-8654
http://www.nationalcitymortgage.com/service_assistanc
e.asp

NATIONPOINT LOAN SERVICES
Call with mortgage questions: 1-800-346-6437
https://carenet.fnfismd.com/nationpoint/
http://www.viewmyloan.com/nationpoint

NATION STAR MORTGAGE
Call with mortgage questions: 1-888-512-2432
Send an email with mortgage questions to:
response.hotline@nationstarmail.com
http://www.nationstarmtg.com/

OCWEN LOAN SERVICING, LLC
Call with mortgage questions: 1-800-746-2936
Home Preservation Number: 866-513-2954
http://www.Ocwen.com
https://www.ocwencustomers.com/csc_fa.cfm

REGIONS BANK
Call with mortgage questions: 800-986-2462
Home Preservation Number: 800-748-9498

http://www.regions.com/
http://regions.com/mortgage/payment_hardship.rf

SAXON MORTGAGE SERVICES, INC./MORGAN STANLEY

Call with mortgage questions: 1-888-649-4816
888-325-3502
http://www.saxononline.com/Home/

SELECT PORTFOLIO SERVICING

Call with mortgage questions: 1-866-662-0035
Home Preservation Number: 888-818-6032
https://www.spservicing.com
https://www.spservicing.com/services/customer/loanres
olution.htm

SUNTRUST MORTGAGE

800-786-8787
Home Preservation Number: 800-443-1032
http://www.suntrustmortgage.com/
http://www.suntrustmortgage.com/loanofficer.asp?hope
now

TAYLOR, BEAN & WHITAKER

888-225-2164
Home Preservation Number: 800-530-2602
http://www.taylorbean.com/

THIRD FEDERAL SAVINGS & LOAN

http://www.thirdfederal.com/

U.S. BANK CONSUMER FINANCE/RETAIL/HOME MORTGAGE

Call with mortgage questions: 1-888-456-2622
Send an email with mortgage questions to:
customerassistance@usbank.com
Call with mortgage questions: 1-800-626-6624

http://www.usbank.com/cgi_w/cfm/personal/products_
and_services/mortgage/home_mortgage.cfm

WACHOVIA MORTGAGE CORP/WORLD SAVINGS
https://www.wachovia.com/foundation/v/index.jsp?vgn
extoid=c96d6344db1dc110VgnVCM100000127d6fa2RCRD

WASHINGTON MUTUAL BANK (NOW A PART OF CHASE, SEE CONTACT INFO ABOVE)
Call with mortgage questions: 866-926-8937
http://www.wamu.com/

WELLS FARGO HOME MORTGAGE
Call with mortgage questions: 1-800-678-7986
Home Preservation Number: 877-216-8448
800-416-1472
www.wellsfargo.com/homeassist
http://www.wellsfargo.com/
https://www.wellsfargo.com/mortgage/account/paymen
thelp

WELLS FARGO FINANCIAL
800-275-9254
http://financial.wellsfargo.com/
http://financial.wellsfargo.com/consumer/paymenthelp
/index.html

At the time of publication, this was the most accurate
lender contact information. Please check your lender's
website for the most update addresses, phone numbers,
and fax numbers and double check with your lender by
phone, as well.

For the most up to date list of lenders, please visit Making Home Affordable:
www.making-homes-affordable.com

GOVERNMENT CONTACTS

FANNIEMAE
http://www.fanniemae.com/kb/index?page=home
http://www.fanniemae.com/kb/index?page=home&c=homeowners_moreoptions
1-800-732-6643

FREDDIE MAC
http://www.freddiemac.com/
http://www.freddiemac.com/avoidforeclosure/home_affordable_mod.html
(703) 903-2000
Toll free: 1-800-424-5401

HUD Foreclosure Counseling
http://www.hud.gov/offices/hsg/sfh/hcc/fc/
(800) CALL-FHA or (800) 225-5342

He Said, She Said:
The Loan Modification Conversation Log

Use this handy log to record all of your communications with your bank. It will avoid errors and confusion on their part and provide you with additional empowerment! Prior to calling, please print out this form and take note of your account number and any questions you may have. You'll be given a lot of information during your conversations. It's a good idea to take notes for future reference.

CONVERSATION LOG

Property Address:

_____

_____

SSN: _____
DOB: _____
PHONE: _____

Bank Name: _____ **Loan#:** _____

Date	Number Dialed	Employee/ Person Spoke With	Conversation Notes	Actions to take?

*Full notes tracking/task manager capability available on www.theloanmodguru.com - Do It Yourself System.

CONVERSATION LOG

Property Address:

_____

_____

SSN: _____

DOB:_____

PHONE: _____

Bank Name: _____ Loan#:_____

Date	Number Dialed	Employee/ Person Spoke With	Conversation Notes	Actions to take?

*Full notes tracking/task manager capability available on www.theloanmodguru.com - Do It Yourself System.

ANOTHER CONVERSATION LOG OPTION

This form can be used to record conversations with your bank. You may want to use this form for your first call, and then use it in tandem with the other conversation log.

Be prepared for the first call to your bank. Take a deep breath, relax, and do your homework before getting on the phone. You will need to have your loan information and your questions, but perhaps what is most important on this first call is that you need to state your case. What is your situation? Why do you want to apply for loan modification? Remember, you don't know who is going to answer your call, what their attitude will be like, or the extent of their knowledge, so keep it short and sweet, but make your point!

For Your First Call

Write down your loan number:_____

Phone number for the bank: _____

Date of your phone call:_____

Name of the bank representative that you are speaking with:

_____

What do you want to say to the bank representative? Briefly, clearly, and concisely explain your situation, your reasons for calling; ask what your loan modification options are:_____

_____

_____

_____

_____

_____

Prepare questions before your call – what do you want to ask the bank? For example, ask the bank representative to describe the application process, the timeline involved, requirements/ documentation, etc.:

_____
_____
_____
_____

Notes / Things to do (i.e., gather tax information, employer information.):

_____
_____
_____
_____

Follow-up questions (i.e., what proof of self-employment do you need?):

_____
_____
_____
_____
_____

Use this form for subsequent conversations:

Write down your loan number:_____

Phone number for the bank:_____

Date of your phone call:_____

Name of the bank representative that you are speaking with:_____

Prepared questions:

_____

_____

_____

_____

Notes / Things to do (i.e., gather tax information, employer information.):

_____

_____

_____

_____

Follow-up questions (i.e., what proof of self-employment do you need?):

_____

_____

_____

_____

_____

BANK STATEMENT ANALYSIS WORKSHEET

Borrower Name: _____

Date		Date	
1. ____	_____	1. ____	_____
2. ____	_____	2. ____	_____
3. ____	_____	3. ____	_____
4. ____	_____	4. ____	_____
5. ____	_____	5. ____	_____
6. ____	_____	6. ____	_____
7. ____	_____	7. ____	_____
8. ____	_____	8. ____	_____
9. ____	_____	9. ____	_____
10. ____	_____	10. ____	_____
11. ____	_____	11. ____	_____
12. ____	_____	12. ____	_____

SAMPLE LETTERS

EXAMPLES OF LETTERS YOU CAN USE TO SAVE YOUR HOME

Don't Forget:

- Keep a copy of all correspondence sent for your personal files
- Fax the letter
- Send the letter by Certified Mail
- Call to follow up and make sure it has been received.

SAMPLE LETTER #1
Urgent Issue and Appeal for Processing Investigation/Escalation

Dear Executive Team:

I have received a denial for incomplete documentation where (Bank Name) requested additional documentation but only gave me 8 days to submit it. Often, the borrowers cannot easily obtain the documentation requested; i.e., updated profit and loss, updated full packages due to untimely (Bank Name) initial processing.

> This letter got the HAMP modification approved after 5 denials!!

I am very confused as to why this is happening as the Treasury Department's HAMP guidelines give a much different directive, as I am sure you are aware:

2.3.3 Incomplete Information Notice

If the servicer receives an incomplete Initial Package or needs additional documentation to verify the borrower's

169

eligibility and income, the servicer must send the borrower an Incomplete Information Notice that lists the additional documentation that the servicer requires to verify the borrower's eligibility. The Incomplete Information Notice must include a specific date by which the documentation must be received, which must be no less than 30 calendar days from the date of the notice. If the documents are not received by the date specified in the notice, the servicer must make one additional attempt to contact the borrower in writing regarding the incomplete documents. This additional notice must include the specific date by which the documentation must be received, which must be no less than 15 calendar days from the date of the second notice. If a borrower is unresponsive to these requests for documentation, the servicer may discontinue document collection efforts and determine the borrower to be ineligible for HAMP. In such an instance, the servicer must send the borrower a Non-Approval Notice.

I appreciate your assistance in checking into this matter.

Sincerely,

SAMPLE LETTER #2
Urgent Appeal and Escalation Based on Use of Inaccurate Self-Employed Income

Date

URGENT APPEAL OF INCOME UNDERWRITING

RE: xxxoooxxx

PROPERTY ADDRESS:

Dear Executive Team:

This letter is to request an administrative review of the above referenced file. According to Heather, the representative from your bank, on (date), I was declined for HAMP due to the use of 14 months worth of bank statements because that is what you have in the file. I asked if you were using the Treasury guidelines to underwrite and calculate income, and the answer was "yes." It is not fair that you calculated my income over 14 months when A) the guideline does not call for 14 months, and B) it does not reflect the accurate income of the borrower, who has been diligent about working to increase his income after the huge economic downturn that caused his hardship and forced him into default. Please reconsider underwriting as requested below.

I am writing to address the Treasury's guidance of self-employed income calculation and respectfully request that the directive under the MHA Handbook v3.1, Section 5.1.2 be used in calculating MY HAMP approval. I have included this guidance here for your review and consideration. It states that 4 months of bank statements be used to back up the profit and loss statement. If we follow this underwriting guidance from the Treasury, my income would pass the NPV test.

5.1.2 Self-Employment Income

If consistent with the Verification Policy, servicers may require up to four consecutive months of bank statements as an alternative to obtaining a profit and loss statement, or if, following receipt, it is determined that the information in the profit and loss statement is insufficient.

Sept 21 – Oct 20   6,970.77

Oct 21 – Nov 18   7,073.75

Nov 19 – Dec 17	7,630.00
Dec 18 – Jan 20	8,350
Jan 21 –Feb 07	4,166 partial month statement

133 days/30 = 4.5 months = 7,597 average deposits; he is keeping his expense factor below 5% and has committed to keeping them at below 5% for 2011.

Sincerely,

SAMPLE LETTER #3
Requesting a Postponement of a Sale Date Due to a Modification Request Being Processed

This is an example of a brief letter you can send to your lender to halt a sale date. Many times their information is either not entered into the system, something is not in sync, etc., or it is your job to provide updates.

URGENT

Written Postponement of Sale Request

Date

Lender Name:
ATT: (If you have a name for someone)
Lender Address:
Lender City, State, Zip

Loan Number:
Borrower Name:
Property Address:
Notice of Trustee Sale Date: (provide the published date)

To Whom It May Concern (or if you have a name):

Please postpone the sale date on the property noted below:

BORROWER NAME:

ADDRESS:

There is a modification request in with your bank. Please search your database to make sure you have received it and escalate the file to a supervisor to have the sale postponed.

This will prevent a costly foreclosure.

Thank you,

SAMPLE LETTER #4
Working With Your Homeowners Association on a Payment Arrangement Sample Letter

Date

HOA BOARD
Attorney at Law (For HOA)
Address
City, State, Zip

RE: HOMEOWNER (Name, Address of unit)

Dear HOA, (Association Name or Attorney)

HOMEOWNER would like to present the following payment arrangement to the Board for a $3,000 balance:

$200 per month on top of the current fees until the debt is paid in full

We are requesting, if possible, to lower some of the fees as HOMEOWNER is having an extreme hardship and may lose the home altogether. Any assistance you can provide to waive some of the fees would be sincerely appreciated so HOMEOWNER can try to retain homeownership and get this all behind her/him/them.

Reminder: Foreclosure hurts the values in the neighborhood for all of your members.

HOMEOWNER does, however, want a full accounting statement directly from the HOA showing the exact fees due and what those fees are due to the discrepancies in the accounting of the amount due.

Sincerely yours,

SAMPLE LETTER #5
Sample Hardship Letter – Three Scenarios

Lender Name:
ATT: (If you have a name for someone)
Lender Address:
Lender City, State, Zip

Loan Number:
Borrower Name:
Property Address

Explanation of Hardship

To whom it may concern:

1. Reduction in Salary/Pay
Due to the current devastating changes in the economy, I have recently received a significant pay cut. I have used almost all of my savings, and it is becoming increasingly difficult to stay up to date on my mortgage payment. As a result of the outlay in expenses and the bleeding dry of my money, I am struggling to make my mortgage payments. Kindly consider my current situation and

provide me with the relief I need to stay afloat. I have every intention of making good on this loan; I just need some relief at this time.

2. Job Loss w/Reduced Income.
Recently, I lost my job due to the shrinkage in the economy. I am actively seeking employment and am confident that I will find a comparable job shortly. Currently, my spouse is still working and our families are assisting us during these trying times. Kindly provide some assistance to us so that we may maintain our home and sustain the possibility of making good on the mortgage we have. We appreciate and thank you in advance for any consideration.

3. Adjustable Rate that has Significantly Increased, Broker Made Unrealistic Promises.

When I received this mortgage, my mortgage broker promised me a low fixed rate mortgage. When I arrived for the closing, my rate was relatively low; however, it was only fixed for a short time. At the closing table, my broker told me the lender would refinance me in two years and pressured me into signing the loan documents. At this time, my rate has risen considerably, and I cannot get a refinance. There is no equity in my home, and the value has dropped tremendously. Please give us some relief with our interest rate. We cannot afford to lose our home that we have worked so hard to keep. Between the increased payment and this tough economy, I just don't see how I will be able to make ends meet without your assistance.

In gratitude,

SAMPLE LETTER #6
Looks Familiar: A Hardship Letter Form From The Banks

Many banks include a Hardship Letter form as part of their branded HAMP package. As discussed, the Hardship Letter gives the homeowner an opportunity to explain the negative changes in their financial situation, and more specifically, why they can no longer afford their current mortgage payment. The following form is modeled after one used by many well-known banks. Consider using a similar letter, as it will be familiar to your lender. Be specific and to the point.

The reason you are experiencing financial difficulties (check the relevant box/boxes):

❐ Income reduction ❐ Self-employed
❐ Unemployed ❐ Divorce
❐ Medical ❐ Other (State a reason):

Please tell us in detail why you are experiencing financial difficulties. If your reasons are medical hardship, for the protection of your privacy, DO NOT describe your specific illness (i.e., cancer, MS, etc.); just describe your illness in general and how it has affected your ability to pay your mortgage (i.e., long-term illness). Attach an additional sheet, if necessary.

Borrower's Signature: Date:
Print Name:
Co-Borrower's Signature: Date:
Print Name:
Loan Number: Phone Number:

SAMPLE LETTER #7
Sample NPV Escalation Letter

Use this sample letter if you were denied HAMP due to your NPV calculation. You have a right to receive the specifics as to how the NPV was calculated. Most of the time, you are not provided with this initially, so you will have to request it.

March 4, 2010

Lender Name
Customer Service Correspondence
ATTN: Executive Team
Lender Address
Lender City, State, Zip

Loan Number:
Borrower Name:
Property Address:

URGENT ASSISTANCE NEEDED – REQUESTING ALL INCOME AND EXPENSE AMOUNTS USED AND THE NPV INPUTS USED IN DENYING MY HOME AFFORDABLE MODIFICATION PROGRAM APPLICATION

DEAR EXECUTIVE OFFICE MHA/HAMP ESCALATION TEAM:

I am writing in reference to Loan #. I was recently notified that this borrower was denied for a HAMP loan modification due to NPV. Per the Treasury guidelines for HAMP, the borrower has the right to have an explanation of what the NPV means, including requesting you to provide the factors used to make the NPV decision.

I hereby request the values used in making the calculations, along with the date the process was completed, within 30 days of the notice of denial, and dates, per that same guideline. I have attached the portion of the Treasury HAMP directive for your review. In addition, I would like a line-by-line explanation of what gross income was used, what expense figures were used, as well as where the value you obtained came from. Was it a BPO, and what amount was it, because the value I have differs significantly from the value figure I was given by the representative.

Why am I getting an in-house modification that is not 31% of my income when I clearly applied and qualify for HAMP?

The HAMP Directive States:

When the borrower is not approved for a HAMP modification because the mortgage loan is deemed NPV negative as outlined in Announcement 09-31, Updates and Clarifications to the Home Affordable Modification Program, the notice must include a list of certain input fields that are considered to reach the NPV result and a statement that the borrower may, within 30 calendar days of the date of the notice, request the date the NPV test was completed and the values used to populate the NPV input fields defined in Attachment 1.

Please also provide the following NPV inputs per supplemental directive 09-08

a. Unpaid balance on the original loan as of [Data Collection Date]
b. Interest rate before modification as of [Data Collection Date].

c.   Months delinquent as of [Data Collection Date]
d.   Next ARM reset date (if applicable)
e.   Next ARM reset rate (if applicable)
f.   Principal and interest payment before modification
g.   Monthly insurance payment
h.   Monthly real estate taxes
i.   Monthly HOA fees (if applicable)
j.   Monthly gross income
k.   Borrower's Total Monthly Obligations
l.. Borrower FICO

Sincerely,

cc: Fannie Mae via email
resource_center@fanniemae.com
Department of Treasury Phyllis Caldwell Chief of Treasury's Homeownership Preservation Office Department of the Treasury 1500 Pennsylvania Avenue, NW Washington, D.C. 20220

SAMPLE LETTER #8
ESCALATION LETTER
Incorrect Assets/Numbers Used

Date

Corporate Headquarters
Lender Name
Customer Service Correspondence
ATTN: Executive Team
Lender Address
Lender City, State, Zip

Loan Number:

Borrower Name:
Property Address:

To Whom It May Concern:

This is an urgent plea to help me concerning Loan # . I have been a very good customer and have always paid my bills on time until I endured a severe hardship with the drop in income due an illness in the family. I was denied for HAMP because I had money in the bank that was used to pay medical expenses and it was NOT savings. I came to you before becoming late, and now I've been put in the position of facing foreclosure because of the HAMP program and the way the trial payments are structured as partial and late.

I am requesting for the third time that I be reviewed for the HAMP program correctly, as under the HAMP treasury guidelines, I am eligible for it. When I resubmitted a few months ago in March, after my denial for HAMP for the above reasons, we provided all of this information in our appeal letter, which was never acknowledged. I am hoping you can help save my family home so I can make a reasonable payment and will do so with your help in providing some payment relief. The traditional modification did not lower my payment. Please help us resolve this issue so I can get properly reviewed for HAMP and get some payment relief.

Please do not forget the Continued Eligibility for HAMP per HAMP Supplemental Directive 10-01:

A borrower who has been evaluated for HAMP but does not meet the minimum eligibility criteria described in the "HAMP Eligibility" section of Supplemental Directive 09-01 or who meets the minimum eligibility criteria but is not qualified for HAMP by virtue of a

180

negative NPV result, excessive forbearance or other financial reason, may request reconsideration for HAMP at a future time if they experience a change in circumstance.

Sincerely yours,

cc: Department of Treasury Phyllis Caldwell Chief of Treasury's Homeownership Preservation Office Department of the Treasury 1500 Pennsylvania Avenue, NW Washington, D.C. 20220
Sigtarp
Barack Obama; White House
Sheila Bair; FDIC
Congressman your state and town
Fannie Mae, Freddie Mac

SAMPLE LETTER #9
HAMP Denial Appeal –
Incorrect Income Figures

Date:

Lender Name:
Customer Service Correspondence
ATTN: Executive Team
Lender Address
Lender City, State, Zip

Loan Number:
Borrower Name:
Property Address:

Dear Escalation Team:

This letter serves as an appeal to the HAMP denial. I have gone over the income numbers that you have used and they are incorrect income figures. I do not believe that the numbers you used reflect a correct NPV denial, rather a denial for too much income, but that income is inaccurate. I would like to be re-evaluated for HAMP with the correct and accurate information. Before I can accept any other modification, I would like to make sure your review for HAMP is accurate because I do not feel that I should be denied for HAMP.

Sincerely yours,

CC: Governor (of your state):
Department of Treasury Phyllis Caldwell Chief of Treasury's Homeownership Preservation Office Department of the Treasury 1500 Pennsylvania Avenue, NW Washington, D.C. 20220

SAMPLE LETTER #10
Sample Request for Assistance from Loan Executive

Date:

MR. COO/CEO
Loan Services
Address:
City, State, Zip

Loan Number:
Borrower Name:
Property Address:

Request for Assistance

Dear CEO,

I know that you are very busy with pressing issues, but I am reaching out to you for assistance in obtaining a HAMP loan modification.

There have been some discrepancies in the application process, and it has taken months to finally get re-reviewed for HAMP because I could not get through to anyone within customer service/loss mitigation to understand what I was requesting. I was not properly reviewed for HAMP, despite three written requests.

I have run my numbers, and I see that I should qualify for the HAMP program according to the guidelines, but I am being told that I don't. I have not been given the opportunity to discuss the discrepancies directly with an underwriter so we can get on the same page, and I fear that although I can make a reasonable payment, I will lose my home if I do not get someone to assist me to resolve this issue.

There is only one income in the household due to family illness, and I also lost my job and had to find another, adding to the stress and hardship on my family. The income that I provided is currently at a housing ratio of 42.92; I was led to understand I need to be over 31% for HAMP and 38% for traditional, which I am - but I was told today, DATE, that I was denied for HAMP because I was already under 31%, which I am not. I requested to speak to the underwriter because it is obvious there is some sort of discrepancy in the numbers.

I have been a great customer up until this hardship, and I can make a reasonable payment. It would be a travesty for my family to lose our home. I anticipate that you will assist in resolving this issue, and I am so grateful for your intervention. I have attached my HAMP proposal for your review and response.

Sincerely
CC: ABC Servicer

SAMPLE LETTER #11
Sample RESPA/Qualified Written Request

Use this example to request all associated documentation – notes, correspondence, etc., for your loan.

Date:

Lender Name:
Customer Service Correspondence
ATTN: Executive Team
Lender Address
Lender City, State, Zip

Loan Number:
Borrower Name:
Property Address:

RESPA QUALIFIED WRITTEN REQUEST

To Whom It May Concern:

Effective immediately, direct all communications via US MAIL.

This is a Qualified Written Request (QWR) as defined by the Real Estate Settlement Procedures Act (RESPA) for information regarding my clients' mortgage loan as referenced above. This is also a request made pursuant to Sections 1641(f) and 2605(k)(1)(D) of Title 15 of the United States Code for the name, address, and

184

telephone number of the holder and owner of the Mortgage Note and for the same information with respect to the Master Servicer of the obligation.

I have reason to believe that the loan terms were misrepresented to us at the time of application and further obscured and/or modified prior to signing. I believe that incomes may have been inflated in the application. I also have reason to believe that certain statements were not provided for approval prior to closing, and that signatures may have been forged on various documents. I am also concerned that certain documents may have not been presented at all. Additionally, I am concerned whether a notary was present to witness client signatures on several pertinent documents and that this transaction did not take place in a legitimate title/escrow/real-estate office, therefore, leaving us ill-advised at the time of closing.

Based on written information I have received on the above-referenced mortgage, I am uncertain as to the identity of the current holder and owner of the original mortgage note. We are, therefore, requesting you to resolve this uncertainty and dispute by providing me with the following information:

A copy of the Note referenced above, showing all endorsements that have occurred, together with any allonge that exists to that Note.

The names of all entities to which the promissory Note referenced above has been sold or otherwise transferred at any time, and the dates that each sale or transfer of the Note occurred.

The names of all entities to which my mortgage or deed of trust has been assigned, and the dates that each assignment occurred. If any assignment in blank has occurred, include it in the list of dates with the notation "In Blank" in place of the name of an entity.

A copy of each of the assignments reflecting each assignment referenced in item five above.

A copy of each written notice that has been sent to me informing me of the sale or transfer or assignment of the Note or mortgage referenced above. You need only include notices sent by you or any corporate affiliate of yours, or notices of which you otherwise have actual knowledge. You need not include any Notice of Transfer of Servicing that may have been sent pursuant to RESPA. This request is only for notices that have been sent in compliance with the Truth-in-Lending Act.

A current statement of all late charges and/or penalties that have been assessed to the account.

Copies of all documents furnished to me at closing, including, but not limited to, the HUD-1 disclosures, TILA rescission notices, statement of finance charges, and any other notice.

Sincerely,

REMEMBER: This letter SHOULD NOT be included with your mortgage payment, but should be sent separately to the customer service address.

You SHOULD continue to make the required mortgage and escrow payment until the request is resolved.

You may bring a private right of action under Section 6, if you suffer damages due to the lender's servicing of the loan. See the RESPA statute and regulations.

http://www.hud.gov/offices/hsg/ramh/res/respareg.cfm

SAMPLE LETTER #12
Sample Escalation and Appeal Request Letter – Incorrect Occupancy Information

Date

Lender Name:
ATT: (If you have a name for someone)
Lender Address:
Lender City, State, Zip

Loan Number:
Borrower Name:
Property Address

URGENT: Denied for inaccurate reasons, home is owner occupied

To Whom It May Concern:

The above-referenced loan was denied for an inaccurate reason. ABC BANK denied this file, stating it was non-owner occupied. This assumption was made because of my tax return and bank statement, and I have an explanation for this. I lived in California with my sister and brother-in-law in the past but never changed my address and did not feel any need to do so. I have provided concrete documentation of my occupancy and have proved that I am the owner occupying the property, including prescription fills, a notarized letter, utility bills, etc.

I would like to get this issue resolved as soon as possible and request an estimate of the time it will take to correct and re-review the previous application for HAMP.

Sincerely yours,

SAMPLE LETTER #13
Escalation for Denial When Not Late

This letter is to escalate when you have been denied for not being late on your mortgage or receive a letter that says not in imminent default.

Date:

Lender Name:
Office of the Chairman
Lender Address
Lender City, State, Zip

Loan Number:
Borrower Name:
Property Address:

HOMEOWNER DENIED FOR ASSISTANCE

Dear CHAIRMAN,

I am in disbelief at the answer I received concerning my HAMP request and would like your assistance.

I recently sent in a HAMP request, and I was denied without real explanation, as per HAMP Guidelines. It was further explained that I was not even considered because I was not 60 days late on the mortgage, which again is contradictory to the HAMP guidelines. Prior to submitting my file, I reviewed the imminent default guidelines with a fine-tooth comb and saw that I was well under the 1.20 calculation below. I am suffering and in need of assistance. I reached out prior to a default because of (add your hardship) causing a hardship. I do not want to be late and ruin my credit standing, but I'm finding it increasingly difficult to keep up with my payment while faced with this financial hardship. I am currently at a (insert your housing debt ratio) housing ratio and the HAMP program could work to bring me to the 31% guideline range without any principal forbearance. I believe I qualify for the program, and I would be able to make that payment even on my reduced income. I am confident that you can help resolve this issue. At this time, I also request a credit hold placed on my account.

HAMP was designed to assist customers who: 1. Have a hardship that makes their current mortgage payment unaffordable; 2. Have a desire to stay in their homes, and 3. Have the ability to make a reduced, but reasonable, mortgage payment.

I look forward to hearing from you soon in resolving this issue.

Sincerely,

Homeowner

*See If You're Not Late on Your Mortgage, Section Seven

LET'S LOOK AT SPECIFIC HAMP CALCULATION EXAMPLES

HAMP EXAMPLES: KNOW YOUR NUMBERS INSIDE AND OUT!

Please note: If investors allow it, in some cases, the lender will permit a partial forbearance of the principal balance. There are new programs that have partial forgiveness/forbearance of the balance.

HAMP Example #1

Original Monthly Payment:

$2,326.21 @ 6.99% for 30 years + 500.00 taxes and insurance = $2,826.27

Monthly Gross Income: $2,000.00

Monthly Property Taxes and Insurance: $500.00

Mortgage Balance: $350,000

Current Property Value: $300,000

Monthly Gross Income X 31% = $620.00 This is the MAXIMUM Total HAMP Payment per the guidelines.

This includes property taxes, homeowners insurance, and HOA, if you have one.

This means you take a $620.00 maximum total payment, minus $500.00 tax and insurance = $120.00

Now your mortgage payment on a $350,000 mortgage is not a realistic expectation.

For example, with a $350,000 Mortgage Balance, Floor Rate 2%, Max Term Extension to 40 Years, the lowest the mortgage only payment can be is $1,059.89 + $500.00 property taxes and insurance = $1,559.89 with this scenario and without any principal forbearance or principal forgiveness.

You can see why at $120.00 for the mortgage only or $620.00 max total payment based on a $2,000.00 gross income, you would fall very short of the guideline as your rate would have to be lowered to negative 7% or the loan balance would have to be lowered to $39,626.76, neither of which is likely to occur.

However, I have seen many homeowners fight numbers like these because they did not do their own calculations to figure out where they were. HAMP calculations can provide an overview of what your particular scenario looks like before you escalate a case that will not make sense to the lender or the investor and does not have the likelihood of being approved.

HAMP Example #2

Original Payment $2,326.21 @ 6.99% for 30 years + 500.00 taxes and insurance = $2,826.27

Monthly Gross Income: $4,000.00

Monthly Property Taxes and Insurance: $237.00

Mortgage Balance: $331,000

Current Property Value: $330,000

Monthly Gross Income X 31% = $1,240.00. This is the MAX Total HAMP Payment per the guidelines, and this includes the property taxes, homeowners insurance, and HOA, if you have one. This means you take $1,240.00 max total payment and subtract $237.00 tax and insurance = $1,003.00

Now your mortgage payment on a $331,000 mortgage is a realistic expectation.

For example:

$331,000 Mortgage Balance, Floor Rate 2%, Max Term Extension 40 Years: the lowest the mortgage only payment can be is $1,002.35 + $237.00 property taxes and insurance = $1,239.35. With this scenario, you are exactly on target, without the need for any principal forbearance or principal forgiveness.

The numbers in this scenario are in line with the guideline and, therefore, have a good chance of being approved for HAMP as long as everything else is in line.

Anna's Recommended Reading for Inspiration and Motivation

Books

The Holy Bible
Who said life didn't come with an instruction manual? I can always find just the right words to get me through ANY and EVERY situation.

BONUS for my readers: FREE BIBLE IN PDF FORMAT AT:
www.theloanmodguru.com/ documents/kjvbible.pdf

The Greatest Miracle in the World, by Og Mandino
This book will remind you of who you are.

Think and Grow Rich, by Napoleon Hill
It is important to know the effects of both positive and negative thoughts on success in life.

You Were Born Rich, by Bob Proctor
A book to help us remember that we are all capable of greatness.

Linchpin, by Seth Godin
A book to give you perspective in the way we must do everything with passion.

The Four Agreements, by Don Miguel Ruis
This is a great nuts and bolts guide on how to view life.

193

Return to Love, by Marianne Williamson
This is a great book to bring peace into your life.

Three Feet from Gold, by Greg S. Reid
This book will remind you to never give up.

Debt Free for Life, by David Bach
A great resource to learn how to cut out additional expenses.

Awaken the Giant Within, by Anthony Robbins
One of the best books to help you to work on your goals.

Use Your Head to Get Your Foot in the Door, by Harvey McKay
Methods to help you find a job.

The Strangest Secret, by Earl Nightingale
Many thousands of people have attributed this recording with turning their lives around and helping them to make their fortunes in the world.

Free MP3 on my site,

www.theloanmodguru.com

Illuminate, by David Corbin
Illuminate shines a light on the negative results of all this positive thinking. It's a story about solving problems by choosing not to ignore them. It's about accentuating the positive while tackling the negative.

The Passion Test - The Effortless Path to Discovering Your Destiny, by Janet Bray Attwood and Chris Attwood

Following your passions is no longer a luxury. In a flat world, it has become a necessity. The good news is, *The Passion Test* is the simple, powerful way to discover your passions and align your life with what matters most to you, starting now.

Affirmations, by Stuart Wilde
Affirmations by Stuart Wilde is not just a collection of nice words to say to yourself; it also serves as a magnificent battle plan, where you learn to expand the power you already have in order to win back absolute control of your life.

A New Earth – Awakening to Your Life's Purpose, by Eckhart Tolle
Tolle describes in detail how our current ego-based state of consciousness operates. Then gently, and in very practical terms, he leads us into this new consciousness. We will come to experience that what we truly are--which is something infinitely greater than anything we currently think we are.

Master Your Debt, by Jordan E. Goodman
This book gives you detailed advice that will help you become debt-free or master the debt you have.

Success Principles, by Jack Canfield
Success Principles has been a major pillar in my life. It can get you from where you are to where you want to be. My teenagers read it, too!

SECTION TEN

SAVE YOUR HOME GLOSSARY

SAVE YOUR HOME
GLOSSARY

I n this section, you will find every mortgage, lending, housing, and modification term. You might be familiar with some of these, but you will surely learn something new!

QUICK TERMS
Loan Types 101

30-YEAR FIXED
The rate remains the same over the life of the loan.

OPTION ARM - NEGATIVE AMORTIZATION LOANS
A mortgage loan which allows you a choice of payments: fully amortizing over 30 years, fully amortizing over 15 years, interest-only payment, or a payment based on a below-market "payment rate" which does not cover even the interest which is due. When only the minimum payment is made, then the difference between what you actually owe and what you are paying is added onto the outstanding loan balance each month and creates what is called "negative amortization."

2, 3, 5, 10-YEAR FIXED
Rate is fixed for a set period of time; then it becomes an adjustable loan.

INTEREST-ONLY LOANS
Only the interest is paid, no portion of the payment goes toward the principal balance owed.

197

ADJUSTABLE TIED TO DIFFERENT INDEXES, SUCH AS LIBOR

Your rate adjusts according to the fluctuation of the index (i.e., Libor, MTA indexes) **it is tied to, plus the margin set forth in your adjustable rate rider.**

Most-Used Acronyms

DTI: DEBT TO INCOME RATIO
A calculation used for qualification purposes.

BPO: BROKER'S PRICE OPINION
Not quite a full appraisal, done usually by a real estate agent.

AVM: AUTOMATED VALUATION MODEL
A computerized property value appraisal.

NPV: NET PRESENT VALUE (please see NPV section)

LOE: LETTER OF EXPLANATION

RMA: REQUEST FOR MODIFICATION AFFIDAVIT FORM

4506
IRS Tax Form to request your tax return transcripts.

VOE: VERIFICATION OF EMPLOYMENT

IO: INTEREST ONLY

Glossary of Terms

203(b): FHA's single family program which provides mortgage insurance to lenders to protect against the borrower defaulting; 203(b) is used to finance the purchase of new or existing one to four family housing; 203(b) insured loans are known for requiring a low down payment, flexible qualifying guidelines, limited fees, and a limit on maximum loan amount.

203(k): This FHA mortgage insurance program enables homebuyers to finance both the purchase of a house and the cost of its rehabilitation through a single mortgage loan.

"A" Loan or "A" Paper: A credit rating where the FICO score is 660 or above. There have been no late mortgage payments within a 12-month period. This is the best credit rating to have when entering into a new loan.

ARM: Adjustable Rate Mortgage: A mortgage loan subject to changes in interest rates; when rates change, ARM monthly payments increase or decrease at intervals determined by the lender; the change in monthly payment amount, however, is usually subject to a cap.

Abandonment: Surrender of property rights with no intention of reclaiming them; mere nonuse is not necessarily abandonment.

Abstract of Title: A historical summary of all of the recorded instruments and proceedings that affect the title of property.

Abstract: A summary; an abridgement. Before the use of photostatic copying, public records were kept by abstracts of recorded documents.

Acceleration: The right of the lender to demand payment on the outstanding balance of a loan.

Acceleration Clause: A provision in a mortgage that gives the lender the right to demand payment of the entire principal balance if a monthly payment is missed. The clause in a mortgage or deed of trust that can be enforced to make the entire debt due immediately if the borrower defaults on an installment payment or other covenant.

Acceptance: The written approval of the buyer's offer by the seller.

Accrued Interest: Interest that has accumulated between the most recent payment and the sale of a bond or other fixed income security. Accrued interest is calculated by multiplying the rate by the number of days that have elapsed since last payment.

Accrued Items: On a closing statement, items of expense that are incurred but not yet payable, such as interest on a mortgage loan or taxes on real property.

Acquisition: Real property acquired by purchase, condemnation, donation, new construction, exchange, or assignment/reassignment by GSA.

Acre: A measure of land equal to 43,560 square feet, 4,840 square yards, 4,047 square meters, 160 square rods or 0.4047 hectares. The (English) acre is a unit of area equal to 43,560 square feet, or 10 square chains, or 160 square poles. It derives from a plowing area that is 4 poles wide and a furlong (40 poles) long. A square mile is 640 acres. The Scottish acre is 1.27 English acres. The Irish acre is 1.6 English acres.

Actual Eviction: The legal process that results in the tenants being physically removed from the leased premises.

Additional Principal Payment: Money paid to the lender in addition to the established payment amount used directly against the loan principal to shorten the length of the loan.

Adjustable-Rate Mortgage (ARM): A mortgage loan that does not have a fixed interest rate. During the life of the loan, the interest rate will change based on the index rate. Also referred to as adjustable mortgage loans (AMLs) or variable-rate mortgages (VRMs).

Adjusted Basis: The original cost of a property, plus the value of any capital expenditures for improvements to the property, minus any depreciation taken.

Adjustment Date: The actual date that the interest rate is changed for an ARM.

Adjustment Index: The published market index used to calculate the interest rate of an ARM at the time of origination or adjustment.

Adjustment Interval: The time between the interest rate change and the monthly payment for an ARM. The interval is usually every one, three, or five years, depending on the index.

Administrator or Administratrix: A person appointed by the court to settle the estate of someone who died interstate.

Ad Valorem Tax: A tax levied according to value, generally used to refer to real estate tax.

Affidavit Of Title: A written statement, made under oath by a seller or grantor of real property and acknowledged by a notary public, in which the grantor (1) identifies himself or herself and indicates marital status (2) certifies that since the examination of the title on the date of the contracts no defects have occurred in the title and (3) certifies that he or she is in possession of the property. (If applicable)

Affidavit: A signed, sworn statement made by the buyer or seller regarding the truth of information provided.

Affordability Analysis: A detailed analysis of your ability to afford the purchase of a home. An affordability analysis takes into consideration your income, liabilities, and available funds, along with the type of mortgage you plan to use, the area where you want to purchase a home, and the closing costs that you might expect to pay.

Amenity: A feature of the home or property that serves as a benefit to the buyer but that is not necessary to its use; may be natural (like location, woods, water) or man-made (like a swimming pool or garden).

American Society of Home Inspectors: The American Society of Home Inspectors is a professional association of independent home inspectors. Phone: (800) 743-2744.

Amortization: A payment plan that enables you to reduce your debt gradually through monthly payments. The payments may be principal and interest, or interest-only. The monthly amount is based on the schedule for the entire term or length of the loan.

Amortization Term: The amount of time required to amortize the mortgage loan. The amortization term is expressed as a number of months. For example, for a 30-year fixed-rate mortgage, the amortization term is 360 months.

Amortize: To repay a mortgage with regular payments that cover both principal and interest.

Annexation: A procedure by which a municipality, such as a city, town, or village, incorporates land within the corporate limits of the municipality; procedures vary depending on state law.

Annual Mortgagor Statement: Yearly statement to borrowers detailing the remaining principal and amounts paid for taxes and interest.

Annual Percentage Rate (APR): A measure of the cost of credit, expressed as a yearly rate. It includes interest, as well as other charges. Because all lenders, by federal law, follow the same rules to ensure the accuracy of the annual percentage rate, it provides consumers with a good basis for comparing the cost of loans, including mortgage plans. APR is a higher rate than the simple interest of the mortgage.

Annuity: An amount paid yearly or at other regular intervals, often on a guaranteed dollar basis.

Application: The first step in the official loan approval process; this form is used to record important information about the potential borrower necessary to the underwriting process.

Application Fee: A fee charged by lenders to process a loan application.

Appraisal: A document from a professional that gives an estimate of a property's fair market value based on the sales of comparable homes in the area and the features of a property; an appraisal is generally required by a lender before loan approval to ensure that the mortgage loan amount is not more than the value of the property.

Appraisal: A written analysis of the estimated value of a property prepared by a qualified appraiser. This is not the same as a real estate tax appraisal done by a town or county.

Appraisal Fee: Fee charged by an appraiser to estimate the market value of a property.

Appraised Value: An estimation of the current market value of a property.

Appraiser: A qualified individual who uses his or her experience and knowledge to prepare the appraisal estimate.

Appreciation: An increase in property value due to changes in market conditions or other causes, which may prove to be either temporary or permanently opposite of depreciation.

Arbitration: A legal method of resolving a dispute without going to court.

As-is Condition: the purchase or sale of a property in its existing condition without repairs.

Asking Price: A seller's stated price for a property.

Assemblage: The combining of two or more adjoining lots into one larger tract to increase their total value.

Assessed Value: The value that a public official has placed on any asset (used to determine taxes).

Assessments: The method of placing value on an asset for taxation purposes.

Assessor: A government official who is responsible for determining the value of a property for the purpose of taxation.

Assets: Any item with measurable value.

Assignment of Deed of Trust: A written document that transfers the beneficial interest in a note and deed of trust from one to another.

Assumable Mortgage: When a home is sold, the seller may be able to transfer the mortgage to the new buyer. This means the mortgage is assumable. Lenders generally require a credit review of the new borrower and may charge a fee for the assumption. Some mortgages contain a due-on-sale clause, which means that the mortgage may not be transferable to a new buyer. Instead, the lender may make you pay the entire balance that is due when you sell the home. An assumable mortgage can help you attract buyers if you sell your home.

Assumption Clause: A provision in the terms of a loan that allows the buyer to take legal responsibility for the mortgage from the seller.

Assumption Fee: The fee paid to a lender (usually by the purchaser of real property) resulting from the assumption of an existing mortgage.

Assumption of Mortgage: Acquiring title to property on which there is an existing mortgage and agreeing to be personally liable for the terms and conditions of the mortgage, including payments.

Attachment: The act of taking a person's property into legal custody by writ or other judicial order to hold it available for application to that person's debt to a creditor.

Attorney-In-Fact: One who holds a power of attorney from another to execute documents on behalf of the grantor of the power.

Attorney's Opinion of Title: An abstract of title that an attorney has examined and has certified to be, in his or her opinion, an accurate statement of the facts concerning the property ownership.

Authorization to Sign as Agent Agreement: Written document given by a beneficiary authorizing an agent to sign a document on their behalf (such as a notice of default).

Automated Underwriting: Loan processing completed through a computer-based system that evaluates past credit history to determine if a loan should be approved. This system removes the possibility of personal bias against the buyer.

Average Price: Determining the cost of a home by totaling the cost of all houses sold in one area and dividing by the number of homes sold.

"B" Loan or "B" Paper: FICO scores from 620 - 659. Factors include two 30-day late mortgage payments and two to three 30-day late installment loan payments in the last 12 months. No delinquencies over 60 days are allowed. Should be two to four years since a bankruptcy. Also referred to as Sub-Prime.

Back End Ratio (debt ratio): A ratio that compares the total of all monthly debt payments (mortgage, real estate taxes and insurance, car loans, and other consumer loans) to gross monthly income.

Back-to-Back Escrow: Arrangements that an owner makes to oversee the sale of one property and the purchase of another at the same time.

Balance: The appraisal principal that holds that value can increase or decrease based on the expectation of some future benefit or detriment produced by the property.

Balance Sheet: A financial statement that shows the assets, liabilities, and net worth of an individual or company.

Balloon Loan or Mortgage: A mortgage that typically offers low rates for an initial period of time (usually 5, 7, or 10 years); after that time period elapses, the balance is due or is refinanced by the borrower.

Balloon Payment: The final lump sum payment due at the end of a balloon mortgage. It also can mean a landlocked parcel of land.

Bankrupt: A person, firm, or corporation that, through a court proceeding, is relieved from the payment of all debts after the surrender of all assets to a court-appointed trustee.

Bankruptcy: A legal proceeding, which allows a debtor to discharge certain debts or obligations without paying the full amount or allows the debtor time to reorganize his financial affairs so he can fully repay his debts. (A bankruptcy does not discharge obligations secured by a deed of trust.)   (See Chapter 7 and Chapter 13 Bankruptcy)

Bargain and Sale Deed: A deed that carries with it no warranties against liens or other encumbrances but that does not imply that the grantor has the right to convey title. The grantor may add warranties to the deed at his or her discretion.

Beneficiary: The lender or their successor in interest for whose benefit a trust is created and to whom the debt is owed.

Bequest: A gift of personal property made in a will. See also Devise. Also, to transfer personal property through a will.

Bid Authorization Letter: Your written authorization instructing the trustee to make the initial opening bid at the trustee's sale on the lender's behalf. This form will also advise of any additional amounts to be included in the opening bid, (total debt), such as funds advanced to pay delinquent real estate taxes, etc.

Bill of Sale: A written document that transfers title to personal property.

Binder: An agreement that may accompany an earnest money deposit for the purchase of real property as evidence of the purchaser's good faith and intent to complete the transaction.

Biweekly Mortgage Payment: A mortgage paid twice a month instead of once a month, reducing the amount of interest to be paid on the loan. The 26 (or possibly 27) biweekly payments are each equal to one-half of the monthly payment that would be required if the loan were a standard 30-year fixed-rate mortgage, and they are usually drafted from the borrower's bank account. The result for the borrower is a substantial savings.

Blanket Insurance Policy: A single policy that covers more than one piece of property (or more than one person).

Blanket Loan: A mortgage covering more than one parcel of real estate, providing for each parcel's partial release from the mortgage lien upon repayment of a definite portion of the debt.

Blanket Mortgage: The mortgage that is secured by a cooperative project, as opposed to the share loans on individual units within the project.

Bona Fide: In good faith, without fraud.

Bond: A real estate bond is a written obligation usually secured by a mortgage or a deed of trust.

Book Value: The value of a property as a capital asset (cost plus additions to value, less depreciation).

Borrower: A person who has been approved to receive a loan and is then obligated to repay it and any additional fees according to the loan terms.

Bridge Loan: A short-term loan paid back relatively fast. Normally used until a long-term loan can be processed or when a seller is awaiting closing proceeds to purchase a new home.

Breach or Breach of Contract: The failure without legal excuse to perform any promise made in a contract. A breach is stated in the notice of default. For example, failure to make payment when it's due.

Broker: A licensed individual or firm that charges a fee to serve as the mediator between the buyer and seller. Mortgage brokers are individuals in the business of arranging funding or negotiating contracts for a client, but who does not loan the money. A real estate broker is someone who helps find a house.

Building Code: Based on agreed upon safety standards within a specific area, a building code is a regulation that determines the design, construction, and materials used in building.

Building Permit: Written governmental permission for the construction, alteration or demolition of an improvement, showing compliance with building codes and zoning ordinances.

Buy Down: A financing technique used to reduce the monthly payments for the first few years of a loan. Funds in the form of discount points are given to the lender by the builder or seller to buy down or lower the effective interest rate paid by the buyer, this reducing the monthly payments for a set time. As an example: The seller pays an amount to the lender so the lender provides a lower rate and lower payments many times for an ARM. The seller may increase the sales price to cover the cost of the buy down.

Buy Down Account: An account in which funds are held so that they can be applied as part of the monthly mortgage payment as each payment comes due during the period that an interest rate buy down plan is in effect.

Buy Down Mortgage: A temporary buy down is a mortgage on which an initial lump sum payment is made by any party to reduce a borrower's monthly payments during the first few years of a mortgage. A permanent buy down reduces the interest rate over the entire life of a mortgage.

Buyer's Agent: A residential real estate broker or salesperson who represents the prospective purchaser in a transaction. The buyer's agent owes the buyer/principal the common-law or statutory agency duties.

Buyer's Broker: A residential real estate broker who represents prospective buyers exclusively, as the buyer's agent, the broker owes the buyer/principal the common-law statutory agency duties.

Budget: A detailed record of all income earned and spent during a specific period of time.

"C" Loan or "C" Paper: FICO scores typically from 580 to 619. Factors include three to four 30-day late mortgage payments and four to six 30-day late installment loan payments or two to four 60 day late payments. Should be one to two years since bankruptcy. Also referred to as Sub-Prime.

Callable Debt: A debt security whose issuer has the right to redeem the security at a specified price on or after a specified date, but prior to its stated final maturity.

Cap: A limit, such as one placed on an adjustable rate mortgage, on how much a monthly payment or interest rate can increase or decrease, either at each adjustment period or during the life of the mortgage. Payment caps do not limit the amount of interest the lender is earning, so they may cause negative amortization.

Capacity: The ability to make mortgage payments on time, dependant on assets and the amount of income each month after paying housing costs, debts, and other obligations.

211

Capital Gain: The profit received based on the difference of the original purchase price and the total sale price.

Capital Improvements: Property improvements that either will enhance the property value or will increase the useful life of the property.

Capital or Cash Reserves: An individual's savings, investments, or assets.

Capitalization: A mathematical process for estimating the value of a property using a proper rate of return on the investment and the annual net operating income expected to be produced by the property. The formula is expressed Income (over) rate = value.

Capitalization Rate: The rate of return a property will produce on the owner's investment

Cash-Out Refinance: When a borrower refinances a mortgage at a higher principal amount to get additional money. Usually this occurs when the property has appreciated in value. For example, if a home has a current value of $100,000 and an outstanding mortgage of $60,000, the owner could refinance $80,000 and have additional $20,000 in cash.

Cash Reserves: A cash amount sometimes required of the buyer to be held in reserve in addition to the down payment and closing costs; the amount as determined by the lender.

Casualty Protection: Property insurance that covers any damage to the home and personal property either inside or outside the home.

Caveat Emptor: A Latin phrase meaning "let the buyer beware."

Certificate of Deposit (CD): A specific sum of money deposited into a savings institution for a specified time period, and bearing a higher rate of interest than a passbook account if left to maturity. Does not have withdrawal privileges as does a passbook account. Also called a time certificate of deposit. (T.C.D.) A document written by a bank or other financial institution that is evidence of a deposit, with the issuer's promise to return the deposit plus earnings at a specified interest rate within a specified time period. See adjustable rate mortgage (ARM).

Certificate of Deposit Index: An index that is used to determine interest rate changes for certain adjustable-rate mortgage (ARM) plans. It represents the weekly average of secondary market interest rates on six-month negotiable certificates of deposit. See adjustable-rate mortgage.

Certificate of Sale: The document generally given to the purchaser at a tax foreclosure sale. A certificate of sale does not convey title; normally, it is an instrument certifying that the holder received title to the property after the redemption period passed and that the holder paid the property taxes for that interim period.

Certificate of Title: A document provided by a qualified source, such as a title company, that shows the property legally belongs to the current owner; before the title is transferred at closing, it should be clear and free of all liens or other claims.

Chain of Title: The history of all of the documents that transfer title to a parcel of real property, starting with the earliest existing document and ending with the most recent.

Chapter 7 Bankruptcy: A bankruptcy that requires assets be liquidated in exchange for the cancellation of debt.

Chapter 13 Bankruptcy: This type of bankruptcy sets a payment plan between the borrower and the creditor monitored by the court. The homeowner can keep the property, but must make payments according to the court's terms within a 3 to 5 year period.

Charge-Off: The portion of principal and interest due on a loan that is written off when deemed to be uncollectible.

Clear Title: A property title that has no defects. Properties with clear titles are marketable for sale.

Closing: The final step in property purchase where the title is transferred from the seller to the buyer. Closing occurs at a meeting between the buyer, seller, settlement agent, and other agents. At the closing, the seller receives payment for the property. Also known as settlement.

Closing Costs: Fees for final property transfer not included in the price of the property. Typical closing costs include charges for the mortgage loan, such as origination fees, discount points, appraisal fee, survey, title insurance, legal fees, real estate professional fees, prepayment of taxes and insurance, and real estate transfer taxes. A common estimate of a Buyer's closing costs is 2 to 4 percent of the purchase price of the home. A common estimate for Seller's closing costs is 3 to 9 percent.

Closing Statement: The statement that lists the financial settlement between the buyer and the seller, and also the costs each must pay. A separate statement for buyer and seller is sometimes prepared. See HUD-1 statement.

Cloud on the Title: Any document, claim, unreleased lien or encumbrance that may impair the title to real property or make the title doubtful; usually revealed by a title search and removed by either quitclaim deed or suit to quiet title. Any conditions revealed by a title search that adversely affect the title to real estate. Usually clouds on title cannot be removed except by a quitclaim deed, release, or court action.

Codicil: A supplement or an addition to a will, executed with the same formalities as a will, that normally does not revoke the entire will.

Coinsurance: A sharing of insurance risk between the insurer and the insured. Coinsurance depends on the relationship between the amount of the policy and a specified percentage of the actual value of the property insured at the time of the loss.

Coinsurance Clause: A clause in insurance policies covering real property that requires the policy-holder to maintain fire insurance coverage generally equal to at least 80% of the property's actual replacement cost. A provision in a hazard insurance policy that states the amount of coverage that must be maintained — as a percentage of the total value of the property — for the insured to collect the full amount of a loss.

Collateral: Property put up by someone getting a loan. If they fail to repay the loan, the property goes to the person granting the loan. An asset (such as a car or a home) that guarantees the repayment of a loan. The borrower risks losing the asset if the loan is not repaid according to the terms of the loan contract.

Co-Maker: A person who signs a promissory note along with the borrower. A co-maker's signature guarantees that the loan will be repaid, because the borrower and the co-maker are equally responsible for the repayment.

Commission: The fee charged by a broker or agent for negotiating a real estate or loan transaction. A commission is generally a percentage of the price of the property or loan. Payment to a broker for services rendered, such as in the sale or purchase of real property; usually a percentage of the selling price of the property.

Commitment Letter: A formal offer by a lender stating the terms under which it agrees to lend money to a home buyer. Also known as a "loan commitment."

Common Area Assessments: Levies against individual unit owners in a condominium or planned unit development (PUD) project for additional capital to defray homeowners' association costs and expenses and to repair, replace, maintain, improve, or operate the common areas of the project.

Common Areas: Those portions of a building, land, and amenities owned (or managed) by a planned unit development (PUD) or condominium project's homeowners' association (or a cooperative project's cooperative corporation) that are used by all of the unit owners, who share in the common expenses of their operation and maintenance. Common areas include swimming pools, tennis courts, and other recreational facilities, as well as common corridors of buildings, parking areas, means of ingress and egress, etc.

Community Land Trust Mortgage Option: An alternative financing option that enables low- and moderate-income home buyers to purchase housing that has been improved by a nonprofit Community Land Trust and to lease the land on which the property stands.

Community Property: A system of property ownership based on the theory that each spouse has an equal interest in the property acquired by the efforts of either spouse during marriage. In some western and southwestern states, a form of ownership under which property acquired during a marriage is presumed to be owned jointly unless acquired as separate property of either spouse.

Community Seconds®: An alternative financing option for low- and moderate-income households under which an investor purchases a first mortgage that has a subsidized second mortgage behind it. The second mortgage may be issued by a state, county, or local housing agency, foundation, or nonprofit organization. Payment on the second mortgage is often deferred and carries a very low interest rate (or no interest rate at all). Part of the debt may be forgiven.

Comparables (COMPS): An abbreviation for "comparable properties"; used for comparative purposes in the appraisal process. Comparables are properties like the property under consideration; they have reasonably the same size, location, and amenities and have recently been sold. Comparables help the appraiser determine the approximate fair market value of the subject property. Properties used in an appraisal report that are substantially equivalent to the subject property.

Comparative Market Analysis (CMA): A property evaluation that determines property value by comparing similar properties sold within the last year.

Compensating Factors: Factors that show the ability to repay a loan based on less traditional criteria, such as employment, rent, and utility payment history.

Compound Interest: Interest paid on the accumulated interest as well as the principal. Interest paid on the original principal balance and on the accrued and unpaid interest.

Computerized Loan Origination (CLO) System: An electronic network for handling loan applications through remote computer terminals linked to various lenders' computers.

Condemn: The taking of privately owned land for public use by eminent domain. In the U.S., just compensation must be provided for any lands thus taken.

Condemnation: Acquisition of real estate through conversion to public use under the right of eminent domain. The acquisition of real estate not being offered for sale that is necessary for government operations by its superior ("eminent") authority over the land ("domain"). Condemnation results in passage of title and land to the government with or without the consent of the landowner, but with just compensation paid to the landowner. The purchase price is determined during the condemnation proceedings. The determination that a building is not fit for use or is dangerous and must be destroyed; the taking of private property for a public purpose through an exercise of the right of eminent domain.

Conditional Line: An agreed line between neighbors that has not been surveyed, or which has been surveyed but not granted.

Conditional-Use Permit: Written governmental permission allowing a use inconsistent with zoning but necessary for the common good, such as locating an emergency medical facility in a predominantly residential area.

Condominium: A form of ownership in which individuals purchase and own a unit of housing in a multi-unit complex. The owner also shares financial responsibility for common areas.

Conforming Loan: A loan that does not exceed Fannie Mae's and Freddie Mac's loan limits. Freddie Mac and Fannie Mae loans are referred to as conforming loans.

Consideration: An item of value given in exchange for a promise or act.

Consideration: Compensation or an equivalent (such as money, material, or services) that is given for something acquired or promised. This may be the appraised fair market value of the real property; or may include protection of the real property against loss by fire, water, or other causes; or any mutually agreeable arrangement that does not conflict with governing statutory limitations. Where the government has a lessor interest, normally the government will consent to the granting of an easement by the owner of the underlying fee, subject to whatever conditions are required to protect the government's interest; consideration is not required. The money (or other property) used to purchase land.

Construction: Erecting, installing, or assembling a new facility. Adding to, altering, expanding, converting, or replacing an existing facility. Moving a facility from one installation to another. Construction includes: Equipment that personnel install on the facility. Site preparation, excavation, filling, landscaping, or other improvements that personnel make to the land.

Construction Loan: A short-term loan to finance the cost of building a new home. The lender pays the builder based on milestones accomplished during the building process. For example, once a sub-contractor pours the foundation and inspectors approve it, the lender will pay for their service.

Contingency: A clause in a purchase contract outlining conditions that must be fulfilled before the contract is executed. Both buyer or seller may include contingencies in a contract, but both parties must accept the contingency.

Contingent Beneficiary: One who, under the terms of a will or trust, may or may not share in the estate upon the happening of an uncertain event. Example: A leaves property to B when B reaches 30, stipulating that if B dies before 30, property goes to C. C is the contingent beneficiary.

Contract: A legally enforceable promise or set of promises that must be preformed and for which, if a breach of the promise occurs, the law provides a remedy. A contract may be either unilateral, by which only one party is bound to act, or bilateral, by which all

220

parties to the instrument are legally bound to act as prescribed. An agreement between two or more persons or entities which creates or modifies a legal relationship. Generally based upon offer and acceptance. An oral or written agreement to do or not to do a certain thing.

Conventional Loan: A private sector loan, one that is not guaranteed or insured by the U.S. government.

Conventional Mortgage: A mortgage or deed of trust not obtained under a government insured program, (such as F.H.A. or V.A.), meaning it is not insured or guaranteed by the federal government.

Conversion Clause: A provision in some ARMs allowing it to change to a fixed-rate loan at some point during the term. Usually, conversions are allowed at the end of the first adjustment period. At the time of the conversion, the new fixed rate is generally set at one of the rates then prevailing for fixed-rate mortgages. There may be additional cost for this clause.

Convertible ARM: An adjustable-rate mortgage that provides the borrower the ability to convert to a fixed-rate within a specified time.

Conveyance: A term used to refer to any document that transfers title to real property. The term is also used in describing the act of transferring.

Cooperative (Co-op): Residents purchase stock in a cooperative corporation that owns a structure; each stockholder is then entitled to live in a specific unit of the structure and is responsible for paying a portion of the loan.

Co-Ownership: Title ownership held by two or more persons.

Cost Approach: The process of estimating the value of a property by adding the estimated land value the appraiser's estimate of the reproduction or replacement cost of the building, less depreciation.

Cost Of Funds Index (COFI): An index that is used to determine interest rate changes for certain adjustable-rate mortgage (ARM) plans. It represents the weighted-average cost of savings, borrowings, and advances of the 11th District members of the Federal Home Loan Bank of San Francisco. See adjustable-rate mortgage (ARM).

Counter Offer: A rejection to all or part of a purchase offer that negotiates different terms to reach an acceptable sales contract.

Covenants: Legally enforceable terms that govern the use of property. These terms are transferred with the property deed. Discriminatory covenants are illegal and unenforceable. Also known as a condition, restriction, deed restriction, or restrictive covenant.

Credit: An agreement that a person will borrow money and repay it to the lender over time.

Credit Bureau: An agency that provides financial information and payment history to lenders about potential borrowers. Also known as a National Credit Repository.

Credit Counseling: Education on how to improve bad credit and how to avoid having more debt than can be repaid.

Credit Enhancement: A method used by a lender to reduce default of a loan by requiring collateral, mortgage insurance, or other agreements.

Credit Grantor: The lender that provides a loan or credit.

Credit History: A record of an individual that lists all debts and the payment history for each. The report that is generated from the history is called a credit report. Lenders use this information to gauge a potential borrower's ability to repay a loan.

Credit Life Insurance: A type of insurance often bought by mortgagors because it will pay off the mortgage debt if the mortgagor dies while the policy is in force.

Credit Loss Ratio: The ratio of credit-related losses to the dollar amount of MBS outstanding and total mortgages owned by the corporation.

Credit Related Expenses: Foreclosed property expenses plus the provision for losses.

Credit Related Losses: Foreclosed property expenses combined with charge-offs.

Credit Repair Companies: Private, for-profit businesses that claim to offer consumers credit and debt repayment difficulties assistance with their credit problems and a bad credit report.

Credit Report: A report generated by the credit bureau that contains the borrower's credit history for the past seven years. Lenders use this information to determine if a loan will be granted.

Credit Risk: A term used to describe the possibility of default on a loan by a borrower.

Credit Score: A score calculated by using a person's credit report to determine the likelihood of a loan being repaid on time. Scores range from about 360 - 840: a lower score meaning a person is a higher risk, while a higher score means that there is less risk.

Credit Union: A non-profit financial institution federally regulated and owned by the members or people who use their services. Credit unions serve groups that hold a common interest, and you have to become a member to use the available services.

Creditor: The lending institution providing a loan or **credit.**

Creditworthiness: The way a lender measures the **ability of a person to qualify and repay a loan.**

Current Assets: An accounting term meaning cash or those things which can be readily converted to cash, such as short-term accounts receivable.

Current Liabilities Debt: Short-term debts. On a closing statement, an amount charged; that is, an amount that the debited party must pay.

Debtor: The person or entity that borrows money. The term debtor may be used interchangeably with the term borrower.

Debt-to-Income Ratio: A comparison or ratio of gross income to housing and non-housing expenses. With the FHA, the monthly mortgage payment should be no more than 29% of monthly gross income (before taxes), and the mortgage payment combined with non-housing debts should not exceed 41% of income.

Debt Security: A security that represents a loan from an investor to an issuer. The issuer in turn agrees to pay interest in addition to the principal amount borrowed.

Declaration of Default: A written document that instructs the trustee to prepare and record a notice of default and, if necessary, to sell the secured property in order to satisfy the unpaid obligation. This document does not require the acknowledgment of a notary public or recording and is merely retained by the trustee in their foreclosure file.

Deductible: The amount of cash payment that is made by the insured (the homeowner) to cover a portion of a damage or loss. Sometimes also called "out of pocket expenses." For example, out of a total damage claim of $1,000, the homeowner might pay a $250 deductible toward the loss, while the insurance company pays $750 toward the loss. Typically, the higher the deductible, the lower the cost of the policy.

Deed: A document that legally transfers ownership of property from one person to another. The deed is recorded on public record with the property description and the owner's signature. Also known as the title.

Deed-in-Lieu: To avoid foreclosure ("in lieu" of foreclosure), a deed is given to the lender to fulfill the obligation to repay the debt; this process does not allow the borrower to remain in the house but helps avoid the costs, time, and effort associated with foreclosure.

Deed In Trust: An instrument that grants trustee under a land trust full power to sell, mortgage and subdivide a parcel of real estate. The beneficiary controls the trustee's use of these powers under the provisions of the trust agreement. A transfer of property to someone to be held in trust for another. Deeds of trust are used in a number of states instead of a mortgage to secure a loan. The deed of trust names the trustees in whom title is placed as security against failure to meet the terms of the loan.

Deed of Restrictions: Clause in a deed limiting the future uses of the property. Deed restrictions may impose a vast variety of limitations and conditions. For example, they may limit the density of buildings, dictate the types of structure from being used in specific purposes or even from being used at all.

Deed of Trust: A written document describing the real property that is being given as security for the repayment of an obligation.

Default: The inability to make timely monthly mortgage payments or otherwise comply with mortgage terms. A loan is considered in default when payment has not been paid after 60 to 90 days. Once in default, the lender can exercise legal rights defined in the contract to begin foreclosure proceedings.

Defeasance Clause: A clause used in leases and mortgages that cancels a specific right upon the occurrences of a certain condition, such as cancellation of a mortgage upon repayment of a mortgage loan.

Delinquency: Failure of a borrower to make timely mortgage payments under a loan agreement. Generally after fifteen days a late fee may be assessed.

Deficiency Judgment: A personal judgment levied against the borrower when a foreclosure sale does not produce sufficient funds to pay the mortgage debt in full.

Demand: The amount of goods people are willing and able to buy at a given price; often coupled with supply.

Department of Veterans Affairs (VA): An agency of the federal government that guarantees residential mortgages made to eligible veterans of the military services. The guarantee protects the lender against loss and thus encourages lenders to make mortgages to veterans.

Deposit (Earnest Money): Money put down by a potential buyer to show that they are serious about purchasing the home; it becomes part of the down payment if the offer is accepted, is returned if the offer is rejected, or is forfeited if the buyer pulls out of the deal. During the contingency period, the money may be returned to the buyer if the contingencies are not met to the buyer's satisfaction.

Depreciation: A decrease in the value or price of a property due to changes in market conditions, wear and tear on the property, or other factors.

Derivative: A contract between two or more parties where the security is dependent on the price of another investment.

Designate Agent: A license authorized by a broker to act as the agent for specific principal in a particular transaction.

Disclosures: The release of relevant information about a property that may influence the final sale, especially if it represents defects or problems. "Full disclosure" usually refers to the responsibility of the seller to voluntarily provide all known information about the property. Some disclosures may be required by law, such as the federal requirement to warn of potential lead-based paint hazards in pre-1978 housing. A seller found to have knowingly lied about a defect may face legal penalties.

Discount Point: Normally paid at closing and generally calculated to be equivalent to 1% of the total loan amount, discount points are paid to reduce the interest rate on a loan. In an ARM with an initial rate discount, the lender gives up a number of percentage points in interest to give you a lower rate and lower payments for part of the mortgage term (usually for one year or less). After the discount period, the ARM rate will probably go up depending on the index rate.

Diversion: A temporary change in the functional use of all or part of a building, involving no major structural changes or modifications.

Document Recording: After closing on a loan, certain documents are filed and made public record. Discharges for the prior mortgage holder are filed first. Then the deed is filed with the new owner's and mortgage company's names.

Dominant Estate: The land that is served or benefited by the existence of an easement on some other land.

Dominant Tenement: A property that includes in its ownership the appurtenant right to use an easement over another person's property for a specific purpose.

Dower: The legal right or interest, recognized in some states, that a wife acquires in the property her husband held or acquired during their marriage. During the husband's lifetime, the right is only a possibility of an interest; upon his death, it can become an interest of land. A wife's interest in her husband's property, inheritable at his death. English probate law set this at

1/3. "Her thirds" was a phrase used for this. In the U.S., it was common for a woman to formally relinquish her dower claim on land sold by the husband. This further guaranteed that the property was clear of all obligations. In some areas, the lack of a dower relinquishment at the time of sale was proof that the man was single or widowed.

Down Payment: The part of the purchase price of a property that the buyer pays in cash and does not finance with a mortgage. Cash portion paid by a buyer from his own funds as opposed to that portion of the purchase price which is financed.

Dual Agency: Representing both parties to a transaction. This is unethical unless both parties agree to it, and it is illegal in many states.

Due on Sale Clause: A provision of a loan allowing the lender to demand full repayment of the loan if the property is sold.

Duration: The number of years it will take to receive the present value of all future payments on a security to include both principal and interest.

Duress: Unlawful constraint or action exercised upon a person whereby the person is forced to perform an act against his or her will. A contract entered into under duress is voidable.

Early Withdrawal Penalty: A charge assessed against holders of fixed interest rate accounts.

Earnest Money (Deposit): Money put down by a potential buyer to show that they are serious about purchasing the home; it becomes part of the down payment if the offer is accepted, is returned if the offer is rejected, or is forfeited if the buyer pulls out of the deal. During the contingency period, the money may be returned to the buyer if the contingencies are not met to the buyer's satisfaction.

Earnings Per Share (EPS): A corporation's profit that is divided among each share of common stock. It is determined by taking the net earnings divided by the number of outstanding common stocks held. This is a way that a company reports profitability.

Easements: The legal rights that give someone other than the owner access to use property for a specific purpose. Easements may affect property values and are sometimes a part of the deed.

Easement Appurtenant: The right of an owner of real estate to use part of another's land.

EEM: Energy Efficient Mortgage: An FHA program that helps homebuyers save money on utility bills by enabling them to finance the cost of adding energy efficiency features to a new or existing home as part of the home purchase.

Eminent Domain: When a government takes private property for public use, the owner receives payment for its fair market value. The property can then proceed to condemnation proceedings.

Effective Age: An appraiser's estimate of the physical condition of a building. The actual age of a building may be shorter or longer than its effective age.

Effective Gross Income: Normal annual income including overtime that is regular or guaranteed. The income may be from more than one source. Salary is generally the principal source, but other income may qualify if it is significant and stable.

Eminent Domain: The right of a government or municipal quasi-public body to acquire property for public use through a court action called condemnation, in which the court decides that the use is public use and determines the compensation to be paid to the owner. The right of a government to take private property for public use upon payment of its fair market value. Eminent domain is the basis for condemnation proceedings.

Encroachments: A structure that extends over the legal property line on to another individual's property. The property surveyor will note any encroachment on the lot survey done before property transfer. The person who owns the structure will be asked to remove it to prevent future problems.

Encumbrance: Anything that affects title to a property, such as loans, leases, easements, or restrictions.

Endorsement/Datedown: A continuation of the trustee's sale guarantee that reports any changes in the status of the property being foreclosed. Such "date downs" are requested from the title company prior to preparation of the notice of trustee's sale and prior to the trustee's sale.

Equal Credit Opportunity Act (ECOA): A federal law requiring lenders to make credit available equally without discrimination based on race, color, religion, national origin, age, sex, marital status, or receipt of income from public assistance programs.

Equalization: The raising or lowering of assessed values for tax purposes in a particular county or taxing district to make them equal to assessments in other counties or districts.

Equitable Right of Redemption: The right of a defaulted property owner to recover the property prior to its sale by paying the appropriate fees and charges.

Equitable Title: The interest held by a vendee under a contract for the deed or an installment contract; the equitable right to obtain absolute ownership to property when legal title is held in another's name.

Equity: An owner's financial interest in a property; calculated by subtracting the amount still owed on the mortgage loon(s)from the fair market value of the property.

Escape Clause: A provision in a purchase contract that allows either party to cancel part or the entire contract if the other does not respond to changes to the sale within a set period. The most common use of the escape clause is if the buyer makes the purchase offer contingent on the sale of another house.

Escrow: Funds held in an account to be used by the lender to pay for home insurance and property taxes. The funds may also be held by a third party until contractual conditions are met and then paid out.

Escrow Analysis: The periodic examination of escrow accounts to determine if current monthly deposits will provide sufficient funds to pay taxes, insurance, and other bills when due.

Escrow Disbursements: The use of escrow funds to pay real estate taxes, hazard insurance, mortgage insurance, and other property expenses as they become due.

Escrow Account: A separate account into which the lender puts a portion of each monthly mortgage payment; an escrow account provides the funds needed for such expenses as property taxes, homeowners insurance, mortgage insurance, etc.

Estate: The ownership interest of a person in real property. The sum total of all property, real and personal, owned by a person.

Estate Taxes: Federal taxes on a decedent's real and personal property.

Eviction: See "Unlawful Detainer."

Evidence of Title: Proof of ownership of property; commonly a certificate of title, an abstract of title with lawyer's opinion, title insurance, or a Torrens registration certificate.

Examination of Title: The report on the title of a property from the public records or an abstract of the title.

Exclusive Listing: A written contract giving a real estate agent the exclusive right to sell a property for a specific timeframe.

Executor/Executrix: The person named in a will to carry out the terms of the will. See "Administrator." A person named in a will to administer an estate. The court will appoint an administrator if no executor is named. "Executrix" is the feminine form.

Extension Agreement: An agreement (normally written) giving additional time to pay an obligation.

External Depreciation: Reduction in property's value caused by outside factors (those that are off the property).

FICO Score: FICO is an abbreviation for Fair Isaac Corporation and refers to a person's credit score based on credit history. Lenders and credit card companies use the number to decide if the person is likely to pay his or her bills. A credit score is evaluated using information from the three major credit bureaus and is usually between 300 and 850.

FSBO (For Sale by Owner): A home that is offered for sale by the owner without the benefit of a real estate professional.

Fair Credit Reporting Act: Federal act to ensure that credit bureaus are fair and accurate protecting the individual's privacy rights enacted in 1971 and revised in October, 1997.

Fair Housing Act: A law that prohibits discrimination in all facets of the home buying process on the basis of race, color, national origin, religion, sex, familial status, or disability.

Fair Market Value: The hypothetical price that a willing buyer and seller will agree upon when they are acting freely, carefully, and with complete knowledge of the situation.

Familial Status: HUD uses this term to describe a single person, a pregnant woman, or a household with children under 18 living with parents or legal custodians who might experience housing discrimination.

Family Housing: All federally owned structures, including trailers, that may be used for lodging of an individual on a permanent basis.

Fannie Mae: Federal National Mortgage Association (FNMA); a federally-chartered enterprise owned by private stockholders that purchases residential mortgages and converts them into securities for sale to investors; by purchasing mortgages, Fannie Mae supplies funds that lenders may loan to potential homebuyers. Also known as a Government Sponsored Enterprise (GSE).

Fannie Mae's Community Home Buyer's Program[SM]**:** An income-based community lending model, under which mortgage insurers and Fannie Mae offer flexible underwriting guidelines to increase a low- or moderate-income family's buying power and to decrease the total amount of cash needed to purchase a home. Borrowers who participate in this model are required to attend pre-purchase homebuyer education sessions.

FHA: Federal Housing Administration: Established in 1934 to advance homeownership opportunities for all Americans; assists homebuyers by providing mortgage insurance to lenders to cover most losses that may occur when a borrower defaults; this encourages lenders to make loans to borrowers who might not qualify for conventional mortgages.

Federal Tax Lien: An obligation to the United States government as a result of nonpayment of federal income taxes.

Fiduciary: One in whom trust and confidence is placed; a reference to a broker employed under the terms of a listing contract or buyer agency agreement.

Fiduciary Relationship: A relationship of trust and confidence, as between trustee and beneficiary, attorney and client or principal and agent.

First Mortgage: The mortgage with first priority if the loan is not paid.

Fixed Expenses: Payments that do not vary from month to month.

Fixed Installment: The monthly payment due on a mortgage loan. The fixed installment includes payment of both principal and interest.

Fixed-Rate Mortgage: A mortgage with payments that remain the same throughout the life of the loan because the interest rate and other terms are fixed and do not change.

Flood Insurance: Insurance that compensates for physical property damage resulting from flooding. It is required for properties located in federally designated flood areas.

Forbearance: A lender may decide not to take legal action when a borrower is late in making a payment. Usually this occurs when a borrower sets up a plan that both sides agree will bring overdue mortgage payments up to date.

Foreclosure: A legal procedure whereby property used as security for a debt is sold to satisfy the debt in the event of a default in payment of the mortgage note or default of other terms in the mortgage document. The foreclosure procedure brings the rights of all parties to a conclusion and passes the title in the mortgaged property to either the holder of the mortgage or a third party who may purchase the realty at the foreclosure sale, free of all encumbrances affecting the property subsequent to the mortgage. The legal process by which a borrower in default under a mortgage is deprived of his or her interest in the mortgaged property. This usually involves a forced sale of the property at public auction with the proceeds of the sale being applied to the mortgage debt.

Foreclosure (non-judicial): A popular term used to describe the procedure followed in enforcing a creditor's rights when a debt secured by any lien on property is in default; however, the correct term for a "Foreclosure" involving a deed of trust is a "Trustee's Sale Proceeding."

Forfeiture: The loss of money, property, rights, or privileges due to a breach of legal obligation.

Fraud: Deception intended to cause a person to give up property or lawful right.

Freddie Mac: Federal Home Loan Mortgage Corporation (FHLM): A federally chartered corporation that purchases residential mortgages, securitizes them, and sells them to investors; this provides lenders with funds for new homebuyers. Also known as a Government Sponsored Enterprise (GSE).

Front End Ratio: A percentage comparing a borrower's total monthly cost to buy a house (mortgage principal and interest, insurance, and real estate taxes) to monthly income before deductions.

Fully Amortized ARM: An adjustable-rate mortgage (ARM) with a monthly payment that is sufficient to amortize the remaining balance, at the interest accrual rate, over the amortization term.

GSE: Abbreviation for government sponsored enterprises: a collection of financial services corporations formed by the United States Congress to reduce interest rates for farmers and homeowners. Examples include Fannie Mae and Freddie Mac.

Gap: A defect in the chain of the title of a particular parcel of real estate; a missing document or conveyance that raises doubt as to the present ownership of the land.

Ginnie Mae: Government National Mortgage Association (GNMA); a government-owned corporation overseen by the U.S. Department of Housing and Urban Development, Ginnie Mae pools FHA-insured and VA-guaranteed loans to back securities for private investment; as With Fannie Mae and Freddie Mac, the investment income provides funding that may then be lent to eligible borrowers by lenders.

Global Debt Facility: Designed to allow investors all over the world to purchase debt (loans) of U.S. dollar and foreign currency through a variety of clearing systems.

Good Faith Estimate: An estimate of all closing fees, including pre-paid and escrow items, as well as lender charges; must be given to the borrower within three days after submission of a loan application.

Government Mortgage: A mortgage that is insured by the Federal Housing Administration (FHA) or guaranteed by the Department of Veterans Affairs (VA) or the Rural Housing Service (RHS). Contrast with conventional mortgage.

Graduated Payment Mortgages: Mortgages that begin with lower monthly payments that get slowly larger over a period of years, eventually reaching a fixed level and remaining there for the life of the loan. Graduated payment loans may be good if you expect your annual income to increase.

Grant: Transfer of title from the government to the first titleholder of a piece of property. This term is generally used by states and the federal government.

Grantee: An individual to whom an interest in real property is conveyed.

Granting Clause: Words on a deed of conveyance that state the grantor's intention to convey the property at the present time. This clause is generally worded as "convey and warrant," "grant," "grant, bargain and sell," or the like.

Grantor: An individual conveying an interest in real property.

Gross Income: Money earned before taxes and other deductions. Sometimes it may include income from self-employment, rental property, alimony, child support, public assistance payments, and retirement benefits.

Ground Lease: A lease of land only, on which the tenant usually owns a building or is required to build as specified in the lease. Such leases are usually long-term net leases; the tenant's rights and obligations continue until the lease expires or is terminated through default.

Ground Rent: The amount of money that is paid for the use of land when title to a property is held as a leasehold estate rather than as a fee simple estate.

Growing-Equity Mortgage (GEM): A loan in which the monthly payments increase annually, with the increased amount being used to directly reduce the principal balance outstanding and thus shorten the overall term of the loan.

Guaranty: Agreement to pay the debt or perform the obligation of another in the event the debt is not paid or obligation not performed. Differs from a surety agreement in that there must be a failure to pay or perform before the guaranty can be in effect.

Guaranty Fee: Payment to FannieMae from a lender for the assurance of timely principal and interest payments to MBS (Mortgage Backed Security) security holders.

HECM (Reverse Mortgage): The reverse mortgage is used by senior homeowners age 62 and older to convert the equity in their home into monthly streams of income and/or a line of credit to be repaid when they no longer occupy the home. A lending institution, such as a mortgage lender, bank, credit union or savings and loan association, funds the FHA insured loan, commonly known as HECM.

Hazard Insurance: Protection against a specific loss, such as fire, wind, etc., over a period of time that is secured by the payment of a regularly scheduled premium.

Heir: One who might inherit or succeed to an interest in land under the state law of descent when the owner dies without leaving a valid will.

HELP: Homebuyer Education Learning Program: An educational program from the FHA that counsels people about the home buying process; HELP covers topics like budgeting, finding a home, getting a loan, and home maintenance; in most cases, completion of the program may entitle the homebuyer to a reduced initial FHA mortgage insurance premium-from 2.25% to 1.75% of the home purchase price.

Hold Harmless Agreement: Provides an indemnification whereby a private party agrees to be financially liable for damages resulting from injuries to persons or damages to property arising from governmental activities or other causes.

Holdover Tenancy: A tenancy whereby a lessee retains possession of leased property after the lease has expired and the landlord, by continuing to accept rent, agrees to the tenant's continued occupancy as defended by state law.

Home Equity Conversion Mortgage (HECM): A special type of mortgage that enables older homeowners to convert the equity they have in their homes into cash, using a variety of payment options to address their specific financial needs. Unlike traditional home equity loans, a borrower does not qualify on the basis of income, but on the value of his or her home. In addition, the loan does not have to be repaid until the borrower no longer occupies the property. Sometimes called a reverse mortgage.

Home Equity Line of Credit (HELOC): A mortgage loan, usually in second mortgage, allowing a borrower to obtain cash against the equity of a home, up to a predetermined amount.

Home Equity Loan: A loan backed by the value of a home (real estate). If the borrower defaults or does not pay the loan, the lender has some rights to the property.

The borrower can usually claim a home equity loan as a tax deduction.

Home Inspection: An examination of the structure and mechanical systems to determine a home's quality, soundness and safety; makes the potential homebuyer aware of any repairs that may be needed. The homebuyer generally pays inspection fees.

Home Warranty: Offers protection for mechanical systems and attached appliances against unexpected repairs not covered by homeowner's insurance; coverage extends over a specific time period and does not cover the home's structure.

Homeowners' Association: A nonprofit association that manages the common areas of planned unit development (PUD) or condominium project. In a condominium project, it has no ownership interest in the common elements. In a PUD project, it holds title to the common elements.

Homeowner's Insurance: An insurance policy, also called hazard insurance, that combines protection against damage to a dwelling and its contents including fire, storms, or other damages with protection against claims of negligence or inappropriate action that result in someone's injury or property damage. Most lenders require homeowners insurance and may escrow the cost. Flood insurance is generally not included in standard policies and must be purchased separately.

Homeownership Education Classes: Classes that stress the need to develop a strong credit history and offer information about how to get a mortgage approved, qualify for a loan, choose an affordable home, go through financing and closing processes, and avoid mortgage problems that cause people to lose their homes.

Homestead: Land that is owned and occupied as the family home. In many states, a portion of the area or value of this land is protected or exempt from judgments or debts.

Homestead Credit: Property tax credit program, offered by some state governments, that provides reductions in property taxes to eligible households.

Housing Counseling Agency: Provides counseling and assistance to individuals on a variety of issues, including loan default, fair housing, and home buying.

Housing Expense Ratio: The percentage of gross monthly income that goes toward paying housing expenses.

HUD: The U.S. Department of Housing and Urban Development: Established in 1965, HUD works to create a decent home and suitable living environment for all Americans; it does this by addressing housing needs, improving and developing American communities, and enforcing fair housing laws.

HUD1 Statement: Also known as the "settlement sheet" or "closing statement," it itemizes all closing costs; must be given to the borrower at or before closing. Items that appear on the statement include real estate commissions, loan fees, points, and escrow amounts.

HVAC: Heating, Ventilation, and Air Conditioning; a home's heating and cooling system.

Important Notice: A written document required by California law to be a part of the recorded Notice of

Default. This document is completed and attached to the Notice of Default (as page 1) prior to recording. It sets forth the reinstatement amount as of a specific date and contains certain language directed to the borrower and emphasizes the fact that a foreclosure proceeding has been initiated.

Improvement: (1) Any structure, usually privately owned, erected on a site to enhance the value of the property-for example, building a fence or a driveway. (2) A publicly owned structure added to or benefiting land, such as a curb, sidewalk, street or sewer. (3) In addition to land amounting to more than repair or replacement and costing labor or capital (e.g., buildings, pavements, roads, fences, pipelines, landscaping, and other structures more or less permanently attached to the land).

Income Approach: The process of estimating the value of an income-producing property through capitalization of the annual net income expected to be produced by the property during its remaining useful life.

Income Property: Real estate developed or improved to produce income.

Indemnification: To secure against any loss or damage, compensate or give security for reimbursement for loss or damage incurred. A homeowner should negotiate for inclusion of an indemnification provision in a contract with a general contractor or for a separate indemnity agreement protecting the homeowner from harm, loss, or damage caused by actions or omissions of the general (and all sub) contractor.

Index: The measure of interest rate changes that the lender uses to decide how much the interest rate of an

ARM will change over time. No one can be sure when an index rate will go up or down. If a lender bases interest rate adjustments on the average value of an index over time, your interest rate would not be as volatile. You should ask your lender how the index for any ARM you are considering has changed in recent years, and where it is reported.

Inflation: The number of dollars in circulation exceeds the amount of goods and services available for purchase; inflation results in a decrease in the dollar's value.

Inflation Coverage: Endorsement to a homeowner's policy that automatically adjusts the amount of insurance to compensate for inflationary rises in the home's value. This type of coverage does not adjust for increases in the home's value due to improvements.

Initial Interest Rate: The original interest rate of the mortgage at the time of closing. This rate changes for an adjustable-rate mortgage (ARM). Sometimes known as "start rate" or "teaser."

Inquiry: A credit report request. Each time a credit application is completed or more credit is requested, it counts as an inquiry. A large number of inquiries on a credit report can sometimes make a credit score lower.

Installment Loan: Borrowed money that is repaid in equal payments, known as installments. A furniture loan is often paid for as an installment loan.

Installment Note: A note calling for payment of both principal and interest in specified amounts, or specified minimum amounts, at specific intervals.

Instrument: A legal document.

Insurable Title: A property title that a title insurance company agrees to insure against defects and disputes.

Insurance: Protection against a specific loss, such as fire, wind, etc., over a period of time that is secured by the payment of a regularly scheduled premium.

Insurance Binder: A document that states that insurance is temporarily in effect. Because the coverage will expire by a specified date, a permanent policy must be obtained before the expiration date.

Insured Mortgage: A mortgage that is protected by the Federal Housing Administration (FHA) or by private mortgage insurance (MI). If the borrower defaults on the loan, the insurer must pay the lender the lesser of the loss incurred or the insured amount.

Interest: The fee charged for borrowing money. A charge made by a lender for the use of money.

Interest Accrual Rate: The percentage rate at which interest accrues on the mortgage. In most cases, it is also the rate used to calculate the monthly payments, although it is not used for an adjustable-rate mortgage (ARM) with payment change limitations.

Interest Rate: The amount of interest charged on a monthly loan payment, expressed as a percentage.

Interest Rate Buydown Plan: An arrangement wherein the property seller (or any other party) deposits money to an account so that it can be released each month to reduce the mortgagor's monthly payments during the early years of a mortgage. During the specified period, the mortgagor's effective interest rate is "bought down" below the actual interest rate.

Interest Rate Ceiling: For an adjustable-rate mortgage (ARM), the maximum interest rate, as specified in the mortgage note.

Interest Rate Floor: For an adjustable-rate mortgage (ARM), the minimum interest rate, as specified in the mortgage note.

Interest Rate Swap: A transaction between two parties where each agrees to exchange payments tied to different interest rates for a specified period of time, generally based on a notional principal amount.

Intermediate Term Mortgage: A mortgage loan with a contractual maturity from the time of purchase equal to or less than 20 years.

Intestate: The condition of a property owner who dies without leaving a valid will. Title to the property will pass to the decedent's heirs as provided in the law of descent. Having no will. If someone dies intestate, the court appoints an administrator to settle the estate.

Intrinsic Value: An appraisal term referring to value created by a person's personal preferences for a particular type of property.

Invalid: Not legally sufficient; no binding force.

Investment: Money directed towards the purchase, improvement, and development of an asset in expectation of income or profits.

Investment Property: A property that is not occupied by the owner.

Involuntary Lien: A lien placed on property without the consent of the property owner.

Joint Tenancy (with Rights of Survivorship): Two or more owners share equal ownership and rights to the property. If a joint owner dies, his or her share of the property passes to the other owners, without probate. In joint tenancy, ownership of the property cannot be willed to someone who is not a joint owner.

Judgment: A legal decision; when requiring debt repayment, a judgment may include a property lien that secures the creditor's claim by providing a collateral source.

Judgment Lien: A lien on the property of a debtor resulting from the decree of a court.

Judicial Foreclosure: A type of foreclosure proceeding used in some states that is handled as a civil lawsuit and conducted entirely under the auspices of a court.

Jumbo Loan: Or non-conforming loan, is a loan that exceeds Fannie Mae's and Freddie Mac's loan limits. Freddie Mac and Fannie Mae loans are referred to as conforming loans.

Junior Lien: A legal claim upon real property recorded subsequent (or recorded prior but has subordinated) to another legal claim upon the same real property.

Late Payment Charges: The penalty the homeowner must pay when a mortgage payment is made after the due date grace period.

Lease: A written agreement between a property owner and a tenant (resident) that stipulates the payment and conditions under which the tenant may occupy a home or apartment and states a specified period of time.

Lease Purchase (Lease Option): Assists low to moderate income homebuyers in purchasing a home by allowing them to lease a home with an option to buy; the rent payment is made up of the monthly rental payment plus an additional amount that is credited to an account for use as a down payment.

Lease Term: For non-operating leases, the lease term is the fixed non-cancelable term of the lease plus all periods.

Leasehold Estate: A tenant's right to occupy real estate during the term of a lease, generally considered being a personal property interest. A way of holding title to a property wherein the mortgagor does not actually own the property but rather has a recorded long-term lease on it.

Legal Description: A description of a specific parcel of real estate complete enough for an independent surveyor to locate and identify. A property description, recognized by law, that is sufficient to locate and identify the property without oral testimony.

Lender: A term referring to a person or company that makes loans for real estate purchases. Sometimes referred to as a loan officer or lender.

Lender Option Commitments: An agreement giving a lender the option to deliver loans or securities by a certain date at agreed upon terms.

Levy: To assess; to seize or collect. To levy a tax is to assess a property and set the rate of taxation. To levy an execution is to officially seize the property of a person in order to satisfy an obligation.

Liabilities: A person's financial obligations, such as long-term/short-term debt, and other financial obligations to be paid.

Liability Insurance: Insurance coverage that protects against claims alleging a property owner's negligence or action resulted in bodily injury or damage to another person. It is normally included in homeowner's insurance policies.

Lien: A legal claim against property that must be satisfied when the property is sold. A claim of money against a property, wherein the value of the property is used as security in repayment of a debt. Examples include a mechanic's lien, which might be for the unpaid cost of building supplies, or a tax lien for unpaid property taxes. A lien is a defect on the title and needs to be settled before transfer of ownership. A lien release is a written report of the settlement of a lien and is recorded in the public record as evidence of payment.

Lien Waiver: A document that releases a consumer (homeowner) from any further obligation for payment of a debt once it has been paid in full. Lien waivers typically are used by homeowners who hire a contractor to provide work and materials to prevent any subcontractors or suppliers of materials from filing a lien against the homeowner for nonpayment.

Life Cap: A limit on the range interest rates can increase or decrease over the life of an adjustable-rate mortgage (ARM).

Lifetime Rate Cap: For an adjustable-rate mortgage (ARM), a limit on the amount that the interest rate can increase or decrease over the life of the loan. See cap, interest rate ceiling, and interest rate floor.

Limited Power of Attorney: A recorded document which authorizes someone to act as attorney-in-fact in a specific manner for someone else.

Line of Credit: An agreement by a financial institution, such as a bank, to extend credit up to a certain amount for a certain time to a specified borrower.

Liquid Asset: A cash asset or an asset that is easily converted into cash.

Lis Pendens: A recorded notice of pending legal action, which notifies prospective purchases and encumbrances that any interest acquired by them in property litigation is subject to the decision of the court.

Listing Agreement: A contract between a seller and a real estate professional to market and sell a home. A listing agreement obligates the real estate professional (or his or her agent) to seek qualified buyers, report all purchase offers, and help negotiate the highest possible price and most favorable terms for the property seller.

Listing Broker: The broker in a multiple-listing situation from whose office a listing agreement is initiated, as opposed to the cooperating broker, from whose office negotiations leading up to a sale initiated. The listing broker and the cooperating broker may be the same person.

Loan: Money borrowed that is usually repaid with interest.

Loan Acceleration: An acceleration clause in a loan document is a statement in a mortgage that gives the lender the right to demand payment of the entire outstanding balance if a monthly payment is missed.

Loan Fraud: Purposely giving incorrect information on a loan application in order to better qualify for a loan; may result in civil liability or criminal penalties.

Loan Officer: A representative of a lending or mortgage company who is responsible for soliciting homebuyers, qualifying, and processing of loans. They may also be called lender, loan representative, and account executive or loan rep.

Loan Origination: The process by which a mortgage lender brings into existence a mortgage secured by real property.

Loan Origination Fee: A charge by the lender to cover the administrative costs of making the mortgage. This charge is paid at the closing and varies with the lender and type of loan. A loan origination fee of 1 to 2 percent of the mortgage amount is common.

Loan Servicer: The company that collects monthly mortgage payments and disperses property taxes and insurance payments. Loan servicers also monitor nonperforming loans, contact delinquent borrowers, and notify insurers and investors of potential problems. Loan servicers may be the lender or a specialized company that just handles loan servicing under contract with the lender or the investor who owns the loan.

Loan to Value (LTV) Ratio: A percentage calculated by dividing the amount borrowed by the price or appraised value of the home to be purchased; the higher the LTV, the less cash a borrower is required to pay as down payment.

Lock-In: Since interest rates can change frequently, many lenders offer an interest rate lock-in that guarantees a specific interest rate if the loan is closed within a specific time.

Lock-in Period: The length of time that the lender has guaranteed a specific interest rate to a borrower.

Loss Mitigation: A process to avoid foreclosure; the lender tries to help a borrower who has been unable to make loan payments and is in danger of defaulting on his or her loan.

Loss Payable Clause: A clause in an insurance policy, listing the priority of claims in the event of destruction of the property insured. Generally, a mortgagee, or beneficiary under a deed of trust, is the party appearing in the clause, being paid to the amount owing under the mortgage or deed of trust before the owner is paid.

Mandatory Delivery Commitment: An agreement that a lender will deliver loans or securities by a certain date at agreed-upon terms.

Margin: The number of percentage points the lender adds to the index rate to calculate the ARM interest rate at each adjustment.

Market Value: The amount a willing buyer would pay a willing seller for a home. An appraised value is an estimate of the current fair market value.

Marketable Title: Good or clear title, reasonably free from the risk of litigation over possible defects.

Maturity: The date when the principal balance of a loan becomes due and payable.

Maximum Financing: A mortgage amount that is within 5 percent of the highest loan-to-value (LTV) percentage allowed for a specific product. Thus, maximum financing on a fixed-rate mortgage would be 90 percent or higher, because 95 percent is the maximum allowable LTV percentage for that product.

Mechanic's Lien: A statutory lien created in favor of contractor's laborers and material men who have preformed work or furnished materials in the erection or repair of a building.

Median Price: The price of the house that falls in the middle of the total number of homes for sale in that area.

Medium Term Notes: Unsecured general obligations of Fannie Mae with maturities of one day or more and with principal and interest payable in U.S. dollars.

Merged Credit Report: Raw data pulled from two or more of the major credit- reporting firms.

Mitigation: Term usually used to refer to various changes or improvements made in a home; for instance, to reduce the average level of radon.

Modification: When a lender agrees to modify the terms of a mortgage without refinancing the loan.

Modification Agreement: A written document, signed by the beneficiary and the borrower that alters the terms of either the note of deed of trust.

Mortgage: A lien on the property that secures the Promise to repay a loan. A security agreement between the lender and the buyer in which the property is collateral for the loan. The mortgage gives the lender the right to collect payment on the loan and to foreclose if the loan obligations are not met.

Mortgage Acceleration Clause: A clause allowing a lender, under certain circumstances, to demand the entire balance of a loan is repaid in a lump sum. The acceleration clause is usually triggered if the home is sold, title to the property is changed, the loan is refinanced, or the borrower defaults on a scheduled payment.

Mortgage-Backed Security (MBS): A Fannie Mae security that represents an undivided interest in a group of mortgages. Principal and interest payments from the individual mortgage loans are grouped and paid out to the MBS holders.

Mortgage Banker: A company that originates loans and resells them to secondary mortgage lenders, like Fannie Mae or Freddie Mac.

Mortgage Broker: A firm that originates and processes loans for a number of lenders.

Mortgage Insurance: A policy that protects lenders against some or most of the losses that can occur when a borrower defaults on a mortgage loan; mortgage insurance is required primarily for borrowers with a down payment of less than 20% of the home's purchase price. Insurance purchased by the buyer to protect the lender in the event of default. Typically purchased for loans with less than 20% down payment. The cost of mortgage insurance is usually added to the monthly payment. Mortgage insurance is maintained on conventional loans until the outstanding amount of the loan is less than 80% of the value of the house or for a set period of time (7 years is common). Mortgage insurance also is available through a government agency, such as the Federal Housing Administration

(FHA) or through companies (Private Mortgage Insurance or PMI).

Mortgage Insurance Premium (MIP): A monthly payment -usually part of the mortgage payment - paid by a borrower for mortgage insurance.

Mortgage Interest Deduction: The interest cost of a mortgage, which is a tax - deductible expense. The interest reduces the taxable income of taxpayers.

Mortgage Life and Disability Insurance: Term life insurance bought by borrowers to pay off a mortgage in the event of death or make monthly payments in the case of disability. The amount of coverage decreases as the principal balance declines. There are many different terms of coverage determining amounts of payments and when payments begin and end.

Mortgage Modification: A loss mitigation option that allows a borrower to refinance and/or extend the term of the mortgage loan and thus reduce the monthly payments.

Mortgage Note: A legal document obligating a borrower to repay a loan at a stated interest rate during a specified period; the agreement is secured by a mortgage that is recorded in the public records along with the deed.

Mortgage Qualifying Ratio: Used to calculate the maximum amount of funds that an individual traditionally may be able to afford. A typical mortgage qualifying ratio is 28:36.

Mortgage Score: A score based on a combination of information about the borrower that is obtained from the loan application, the credit report, and property value information. The score is a comprehensive analysis of the borrower's ability to repay a mortgage loan and manage credit.

Mortgagee: The lender in a mortgage agreement.

Mortgagor: The borrower in a mortgage agreement.

Multifamily Housing: A building with more than four residential rental units.

Multiple Listing Service (MLS): Within a particular geographic area, realtors submit listings and agree to attempt to sell all properties in the MLS. The MLS is a service of the local Board of Realtors®. The local MLS has a protocol for updating listings and sharing commissions. The MLS offers the advantage of more timely information, availability, and access to houses and other types of property on the market.

National Credit Repositories: Currently, there are three companies that maintain national credit-reporting databases. These are Equifax, Experian, and Trans Union, referred to as Credit Bureaus.

Negative Amortization: Amortization means that monthly payments are large enough to pay the interest and reduce the principal on your mortgage. Negative amortization occurs when the monthly payments do not cover all of the interest cost. The interest cost that isn't covered is added to the unpaid principal balance. This means that even after making many payments, you could owe more than you did at the beginning of the loan. Negative amortization can occur when an ARM has a payment cap that results in monthly payments not high enough to cover the interest due.

Negotiable Instrument: A written promise or order to pay a specific sum of money that may be transferred by endorsement or delivery. The transferee then has the original payee's rights to payment.

Net Income: Your take-home pay, the amount of money that you receive in your paycheck after taxes and deductions.

Net Operating Income (NOI): The income projected for an income-producing property after deducting losses for vacancy and collection operating expenses.

Net Worth: The difference between total assets and liabilities of an individual, corporation, etc., term investments if they withdraw their money before maturity. Such a penalty would be assessed, for instance, if someone who has a six-month certificate of deposit withdrew the money after four months. The value of all of a person's assets, including cash, minus all liabilities.

No Cash Out Refinance: A refinance of an existing loan only for the amount remaining on the mortgage. The borrower does not get any cash against the equity of the home. Also called a "rate and term refinance."

No Cost Loan: There are many variations of a no cost loan. Generally, it is a loan that does not charge for items such as title insurance, escrow fees, settlement fees, appraisal, recording fees or notary fees. It may also offer no points. This lessens the need for upfront cash during the buying process; however, no cost loans have a higher interest rate.

Nonperforming Asset: An asset such as a mortgage that is not currently accruing interest or which interest is not being paid.

Nonmilitary Affidavits: A sworn statement, in writing from the beneficiary or his agent which declares that the property owner is not entitled to any rights under the Soldiers and Sailors Civil Relief Act of 1940.

Notary Public: A person who serves as a public official and certifies the authenticity of required signatures on a document by signing and stamping the document.

Note: A legal document (promise to pay), obligating a borrower to repay a mortgage loan at a stated interest rate over a specified period of time.

Note Rate: The interest rate stated on a mortgage note.

Notice of Default: A written document that gives constructive notice of a trustor's failure to perform his obligation under a deed of trust. This document does not require the acknowledgment of a notary public and must be recorded.

Notice of Default: A formal written notice to a borrower that there is a default on a loan and that legal action is possible.

Notice of Rescission: A written document that cancels or annuls the effect of a notice of default when a default has been cured (reinstated). This document does not require the acknowledgment of a notary public, but must be recorded with the county recorder in the county in which the property is located.

Notice of Trustee's Sale: A written document that sets forth the day, date, and time of the trustee's sale, describes the property to be sold and gives an estimate of the unpaid debt as of the first publication debt. This document is prepared by the trustee and does not require the acknowledgment of a notary public and must be recorded with the county recorder in the county in which the property is located at least 14 days prior to the scheduled sale date. The notice of trustee's sale to be published in a qualified newspaper in the city (or judicial district), in which the property is located. This publication must appear for 3 consecutive weeks, with the first publication date being at least 20 days prior to the sale date.

Notional Principal Amount: The proposed amount which interest rate swap payments are based, but generally not paid or received by either party.

Non-Conforming Loan: A loan that exceeds Fannie Mae's and Freddie Mac's loan limits. Freddie Mac and Fannie Mae loans are referred to as conforming loans.

Offer: Indication by a potential buyer of a willingness to purchase a home at a specific price; generally put forth in writing.

Original Principal Balance: The total principal owed on a mortgage prior to any payments being made.

Origination: The process of preparing, submitting, and evaluating a loan application; generally includes a credit check, verification of employment, and a property appraisal.

Origination Fee: The charge for originating a loan; is usually calculated in the form of points and paid at closing. One point equals one percent of the loan amount. On a conventional loan, the loan origination fee is the number of points a borrower pays.

Owner Financing: A home purchase where the seller provides all or part of the financing, acting as a lender.

Ownership: Ownership is documented by the deed to a property. The type or form of ownership is important if there is a change in the status of the owners or if the property changes ownership.

Owner's Policy: The insurance policy that protects the buyer from title defects.

PITI: Principal, Interest, Taxes, and Insurance: The four elements of a monthly mortgage payment; payments of principal and interest go directly toward repaying the loan, while the portion that covers taxes and insurance (homeowner's and mortgage, if applicable) goes into an escrow account to cover the fees when they are due.

PITI Reserves: A cash amount that a borrower must have on hand after making a down payment and paying all closing costs for the purchase of a home. The principal, interest, taxes, and insurance (PITI) reserves must equal the amount that the borrower would have to pay for PITI for a predefined number of months.

PMI: Private Mortgage Insurance; privately-owned companies that offer standard and special affordable mortgage insurance programs for qualified borrowers with down payments of less than 20% of a purchase price.

Package Loan: A real estate loan used to finance the purchase of both real property and personal property, such as in the purchase of a new home that includes carpeting, window coverings, and major appliances.

Partial Claim: A loss mitigation option offered by the FHA that allows a borrower, with help from a lender, to get an interest-free loan from HUD to bring their mortgage payments up to date.

Partial Payment: A payment that is less than the total amount owed on a monthly mortgage payment. Normally, lenders do not accept partial payments. The lender may make exceptions during times of difficulty. Contact your lender prior to the due date if a partial payment is needed.

Participation Mortgage: A mortgage loan wherein the lender has a partial equity interest in the property or receives a portion of the income from the property.

Payment Cap: A limit on how much an ARM's payment may increase, regardless of how much the interest rate increases.

Payment Change Date: The date when a new monthly payment amount takes effect on an adjustable-rate mortgage (ARM) or a graduated-payment mortgage (GPM). Generally, the payment change date occurs in the month immediately after the interest rate adjustment date.

Payment Due Date: Contract language specifying when payments are due on money borrowed. The due date is always indicated and means that the payment must be received on or before the specified date. Grace periods prior to assessing a late fee or additional interest do not eliminate the responsibility of making payments on time.

Payoff Statement: The document signed by a lender indicating the amount required to pay a loan balance in full and satisfy the debt; used in the settlement process to protect both the seller's and the buyers interest.

Daily Periodic Payment Cap: For an adjustable-rate mortgage (ARM), a limit on the amount those payments can increase or decrease during any one adjustment period.

Periodic Rate Cap: For an adjustable-rate mortgage (ARM), a limit on the amount that the interest rate can increase or decrease during any one adjustment period, regardless of how high or low the index might be.

Perils: For homeowner's insurance, an event that can damage the property. Homeowner's insurance may cover the property for a wide variety of perils caused by accidents, nature, or people.

Personal Property: Any property that is not real property or attached to real property. For example, furniture is not attached; however, a new light fixture would be considered attached and part of the real property.

Physical Deterioration: A reduction in a property's values resulting from a decline in physical condition; can be caused by action of the elements or by ordinary wear and tear.

Planned Unit Development (PUD): A development that is planned and constructed as one entity. Generally, there are common features in the homes or lots governed by covenants attached to the deed. Most planned developments have common land and facilities owned and managed by the owner's or neighborhood association. Homeowners usually are required to participate in the association via a payment of annual dues.

Points: A point is equal to one percent of the principal amount of your mortgage. For example, if you get a mortgage for $95,000, one point means you pay $950 to the lender. Lenders frequently charge points in both fixed-rate and adjustable-rate mortgages in order to increase the yield on the mortgage and to cover loan closing costs. These points usually are collected at closing and may be paid by the borrower or the home seller, or may be split between them.

Postponement: A verbal announcement made at the time and place of the scheduled trustee's sale that establishes a new date or time for the trustee's sale. The sale cannot be changed from the originally noticed location.

Power of Attorney: A legal document that authorizes another person to act on your behalf. A power of attorney can grant complete authority or can be limited to certain acts or certain periods of time or both.

Pre-Approval: A lender commits to lend to a potential borrower a fixed loan amount based on a completed loan application, credit reports, debt, savings and has been reviewed by an underwriter. The commitment remains as long as the borrower still meets the qualification requirements at the time of purchase. This does not guaranty a loan until the property has passed inspections underwriting guidelines.

Prearranged Refinancing Agreement: A formal or informal arrangement between a lender and a borrower wherein the lender agrees to offer special terms (such as a reduction in the costs) for a future refinancing of a mortgage being originated as an inducement for the borrower to enter into the original mortgage transaction.

Predatory Lending: Abusive lending practices that include a mortgage loan to someone who does not have the ability to repay. It also pertains to repeated refinancing of a loan charging high interest and fees each time.

Predictive Variables: The variables that are part of the formula comprising elements of a credit-scoring model. These variables are used to predict a borrower's future credit performance.

Preferred Stock: Stock that takes priority over common stock with regard to dividends and liquidation rights. Preferred stockholders typically have no voting rights.

Pre-foreclosure Sale: A procedure in which the borrower is allowed to sell a property for an amount less than what is owed on it to avoid a foreclosure. This sale fully satisfies the borrower's debt.

Preliminary Injunction: A judicial order granted by a judge of the Superior Court, which prohibits the trustee from proceeding with any further action on a specific foreclosure file until a trial is held or settlement reached. This occurs when there is a dispute between the owner of a property and the beneficiary. A Trustee's Sale cannot be held any sooner than seven (7) days from the dismissal of the action or the expiration of a restraining order, injunction, or stay from any court of competent jurisdiction. However, the order or any amendment thereto may expressly provide for an earlier sale date.

Premises: A somewhat fluid term meaning land and its appurtenances, or land and its buildings and structures.

Prepaid Items: On a closing statement, items that have been paid in advance by the seller, such as insurance premiums and some real estate taxes, for which he or she must be reimbursed by the buyer.

Prepayment: Any amount paid to reduce the principal balance of a loan before the due date or payment in full of a mortgage. This can occur with the sale of the property, the pay off the loan in full, or a foreclosure. In each case, full payment occurs before the loan has been fully amortized.

Prepayment Penalty: A provision in some loans that charges a fee to a borrower who pays off a loan before it is due.

Prepayment Penalty Mortgage (PPM): A type of mortgage that requires the borrower to pay a penalty for prepayment, partial payment of principal, or for repaying the entire loan within a certain time period. A partial payment is generally defined as an amount exceeding 20% of the original principal balance.

Pre-Publication Period: The three-month period following the recording of the notice of default. Prior to 1986, this period was called the reinstatement period.

Pre-Qualify: A lender informally determines the maximum amount an individual is eligible to borrow. This is not a guaranty of a loan.

Premium: An amount paid on a regular schedule by a policyholder that maintains insurance coverage.

Present Owner, Current Owner, New Owner: The successor to the trustor named in the deed of trust and now the owner of the property.

Price Range: The high and low amount a buyer is willing to pay for a home.

Prime Rate: The interest rate that banks charge to preferred customers. Changes in the prime rate are publicized in the business media. Prime rate can be used as the basis for adjustable rate mortgages (ARMs) or home equity lines of credit. The prime rate also affects the current interest rates being offered at a particular point in time on fixed mortgages. Changes in the prime rate do not affect the interest on a fixed mortgage.

Principal: The amount of money borrowed to buy a house or the amount of the loan that has not been paid back to the lender. This does not include the interest paid to borrow that money. The principal balance is the amount owed on a loan at any given time. It is the original loan amount minus the total repayments of principal made.

Principal, Interest, Taxes, and Insurance (PITI): The four elements of a monthly mortgage payment; payments of principal and interest go directly toward repaying the loan, while the portion that covers taxes and insurance (homeowner's and mortgage, if applicable) goes into an escrow account to cover the fees when they are due.

Private Mortgage Insurance (PMI): Insurance purchased by a buyer to protect the lender in the event of default. The cost of mortgage insurance is usually added to the monthly payment. Mortgage insurance is generally maintained until over 20% of the outstanding amount of the loan is paid or for a set period of time, seven years is normal. Mortgage insurance may be available through a government agency, such as the Federal Housing Administration (FHA) or the Veterans Administration (VA), or through private mortgage insurance companies (PMI).

Probate: The process of proving a decedent's will and settling the estate. The signing of a will was typically witnessed by neighbors, who would later swear in court that they saw the decedent sign the will prior to death. This "proved" that the will was actually that of the decedent.

Profit & Loss Statement: A statement showing the income and expenses of a business over a stated time, the difference being the profit or loss for the period.

Property (Fixture and Non-Fixture): In a real estate contract, the property is the land within the legally described boundaries and all permanent structures and fixtures. Ownership of the property confers the legal right to use the property as allowed within the law and within the restrictions of zoning or easements. Fixture property refers to those items permanently attached to the structure, such as carpeting or a ceiling fan, which transfers with the property.

Property Tax: A tax charged by local government and used to fund municipal services such as schools, police, or street maintenance. The amount of property tax is determined locally by a formula, usually based on a percent per $1,000 of assessed value of the property.

Property Tax Deduction: The U.S. tax code allows homeowners to deduct the amount they have paid in property taxes from their total income.

Publication Letter: The trustee sends this letter to the lender. When completed and returned, it authorizes the trustee to proceed with the scheduling of the trustee's sale and preparation of the notice of trustee's sale.

Publication Period: This is the interval beginning the day after the pre-publication period expires and ending with the conducting of the trustee's sale. During the publication period, the notice of trustee's sale is published, posted, recorded, and copies are mailed to all entitled parties. The publication period is normally 30 to 40 days.

Public Record Information: Court records of events that are a matter of public interest, such as credit, bankruptcy, foreclosure and tax liens. Creditors regard the presence of public record information on a credit report negatively.

Public Auction: A meeting in an announced public location to sell property to repay a mortgage that is in default.

Public Domain: Land or interest in land owned by the United States and administered by the Secretary of the Interior, through the Bureau of Land Management, without regard to how the United States acquired ownership, except lands located in the Outer Continental Shelf and lands held for the benefit of Indians, Aleuts, and Eskimos.

PUD (Planned Unit Development): A project or subdivision that includes common property that is owned and maintained by a homeowners' association for the benefit and use of the individual PUD unit owners.

Punch List: A list of items that have not been completed at the time of the final walk through of a newly constructed home.

Purchase Offer: A detailed, written document that makes an offer to purchase a property, and that may be amended several times in the process of negotiations. When signed by all parties involved in the sale, the purchase offer becomes a legally binding contract, sometimes called the Sales Contract.

Purchase and Sale Agreement: A written contract signed by the buyer and seller stating the terms and conditions under which a property will be sold.

Purchase-Money Mortgage (PMM): A note secured by a mortgage or deed of trust given by a buyer, as a borrower, to a seller, as a lender, as part of the purchase price of the real estate.

Qualifying Ratios: Guidelines utilized by lenders to determine how much money a homebuyer is qualified to borrow. Lending guidelines typically include a maximum housing expense to income ratio and a maximum monthly expense to income ratio.

Quiet Title: A court action to remove a cloud on the title.

Quitclaim Deed: A deed transferring ownership of a property but does not make any guarantee of clear title.

Radon: A radioactive gas found in some homes that, if occurring in strong enough concentrations, can cause health problems.

Rate Cap: A limit on an ARM on how much the interest rate or mortgage payment may change. Rate caps limit how much the interest rates can rise or fall on the adjustment dates and over the life of the loan.

Rate Lock: A commitment by a lender to a borrower guaranteeing a specific interest rate over a period of time at a set cost.

Real Estate Agent: An individual who is licensed to negotiate and arrange real estate sales; works for a real estate broker.

Real Estate Mortgage Investment Conduit (REMIC): A security representing an interest in a trust having multiple classes of securities. The securities of each class entitle investors to cash payments structured differently from the payments on the underlying mortgages.

Real Estate Property Tax Deduction: A tax deductible expense reducing a taxpayer's taxable income.

Real Estate Settlement Procedures Act (RESPA): A law protecting consumers from abuses during the residential real estate purchase and loan process by requiring lenders to disclose all settlement costs, practices, and relationships.

Real Property: Land, including all the natural resources and permanent buildings on it.

REALTOR®: A real estate agent or broker who is a member of the NATIONAL ASSOCIATION OF REALTORS and its local and state associations.

Reconciliation: The final step in the appraisal process, in which the appraiser combines the estimates of value received from the sales comparison, cost, and income approaches to arrive at a final estimate of market value for the subject property.

Reconveyance: A recorded document, which gives notice that the loan secured by the identified deed of trust has been paid in full.

Recorder: The public official who keeps records of transactions concerning real property. Sometimes known as a "Registrar of Deeds" or "County Clerk."

Recording: The recording in a registrar's office of an executed legal document. These include deeds, mortgages, satisfaction of a mortgage, or an extension of a mortgage making it a part of the public record.

Recording Fees: Charges for recording a deed with the appropriate government agency.

Redemption: The right of a defaulted property owner to recover his or her property by curing the default.

Redemption Period: A period of time established by state law during which a property owner had the right to redeem his or her real estate from a foreclosure or tax sale by paying the sales price, interest, and cost. Many states do not have mortgage redemption laws.

Refinancing: Paying off one loan by obtaining another; refinancing is generally done to secure better loan terms (like a lower interest rate).

Rehabilitation Mortgage: A mortgage that covers the costs of rehabilitating (repairing or Improving) a property; some rehabilitation mortgages - like the FHA's 203(k) - allow a borrower to roll the costs of rehabilitation and home purchase into one mortgage loan.

Rescission: The cancellation or annulment of a transaction or contract by the operation of a law or by mutual consent. Borrowers usually have the option to cancel a refinance transaction within three business days after it has closed. See "Notice of Rescission."

Reinstatement: A curing of a default and restoration of the loan to current status through payment of past-due amounts together with the fee and expenses of the trustee.

Reinstatement Period: This is the interval from the date the notice of default is recorded until five business days prior to the date of sale during which time a default may be reinstated/cured.

Reinstatement Period: A phase of the foreclosure process where the homeowner has an opportunity to stop the foreclosure by paying money that is owed to the lender.

Remaining Balance: The amount of principal that has not yet been repaid.

Remaining Term: The original amortization term, minus the number of payments that have been applied.

Repayment Plan: An agreement between a lender and a delinquent borrower where the borrower agrees to make additional payments to pay down past due amounts while making regularly scheduled payments.

Replacement Cost: The construction cost at current prices of property that is not necessarily an exact duplicate of the subject property but serves the same purpose or function as the original.

Request for Notice: A recorded document which requests a copy of any notice of default and any notice of sale to be sent to the requester at the address shown.

Request to Prepare Notice of Default: See "Transmittal Form."

Restrictive Covenant: An agreement contained in a deed or lease that restricts the use and occupancy of real property.

Return and Account of Sale by Trustee: An itemization prepared by the trustee or his agent and sent to the successful bidder at the sale. It gives a complete accounting of the successful bid.

Return on Average Common Equity: Net income available to common stockholders, as a percentage of average common stockholder equity.

Reverse Mortgage (HECM): The reverse mortgage is used by senior homeowners age 62 and older to convert the equity in their home into monthly streams of income and/or a line of credit to be repaid when they no longer occupy the home. A lending institution, such as a mortgage lender, bank, credit union, or savings and loan association, funds the FHA insured loan, commonly known as HECM.

Right of First Refusal: A provision in an agreement that requires the owner of a property to give one party an opportunity to purchase or lease a property before it is offered for sale or lease to others.

Right of Survivorship: In joint tenancy, the right of survivors to acquire the interest of a deceased joint tenant. See "Joint Tenancy."

Risk Based Capital: An amount of capital needed to offset losses during a ten-year period with adverse circumstances.

Risk-Based Pricing: Fee structure used by creditors based on risks of granting credit to a borrower with a poor credit history.

Risk Scoring: An automated way to analyze a credit report, versus a manual review. It takes into account late payments, outstanding debt, credit experience, and number of inquiries in an unbiased manner.

Sale Leaseback: When a seller deeds property to a buyer for a payment, and the buyer simultaneously leases the property back to the seller.

Sales Comparison Approach: The process of estimating the value of a property by examining and comparing actual sales of comparable properties.

Satisfaction of Mortgage: A document acknowledging the payment of a mortgage debt.

Second Mortgage: An additional mortgage on property. In case of a default, the first mortgage must be paid before the second mortgage. Second loans are more risky for the lender and usually carry a higher interest rate.

Secondary Mortgage Market: The buying and selling of mortgage loans. Investors purchase residential mortgages originated by lenders, which in turn provides the lenders with capital for additional lending.

Secured Loan: A loan backed by collateral, such as property.

Security: The property that will be pledged as collateral for a loan.

Seller Take Back: An agreement where the owner of a property provides second mortgage financing. These are often combined with an assumed mortgage instead of a portion of the seller's equity.

Serious Delinquency: A mortgage that is 90 days or more past due.

Security Deposit: A payment by tenant, held by the landlord during the lease term, and kept (wholly or partially) on default or destruction of the premises by the tenant.

Servicer: A business that collects mortgage payments from borrowers and manages the borrower's escrow accounts.

Servicing: The collection of mortgage payments from borrowers and related responsibilities of a loan servicer.

Setback: The distance between a property line and the area where building can take place. Setbacks are used to assure space between buildings and from roads for many purposes, including drainage and utilities.

Settlement: Another name for closing.

Settlement Statement: A document required by the Real Estate Settlement Procedures Act (RESPA). It is an itemized statement of services and charges relating to the closing of a property transfer. The buyer has the right to examine the settlement statement one day before the closing. This is called the HUD 1 Settlement Statement.

Soldier's and Sailor's Relief Act: An act passed by Congress in 1940, for the financial protection of those persons serving in the military service. This act is the reason for the completion of the nonmilitary affidavit forms.

Special Forbearance: A loss mitigation option where the lender arranges a revised repayment plan for the borrower that may include a temporary reduction or suspension of monthly loan payments.

Special Warranty Deed: A deed in which the grantor warrants, or guarantees, the title only against defects arising during the period of his or her tenure and ownership of the property and not against defects existing before that time, generally using the language, "By, through or under the grantor but not otherwise."

Specific Lien: A lien affecting or attaching only to a certain, specific parcel of land, or piece of property.

Standard Payment Calculation: The method used to determine the monthly payment required to repay the remaining balance of a mortgage in substantially equal installments over the remaining term of the mortgage at the current interest rate.

Statement/Invoice: An itemization of the trustee's fee and expenses incurred at the conclusion of the foreclosure proceeding (cancellation, reinstatement, payoff or completed sale).

Statute of Limitation: That law pertaining to the period of time within which certain instruments, such as deeds, be in writing to be legally enforceable.

Statutory Lien: A lien imposed on property by statute-a tax lien, for example- in contrast to an equitable lien, which arises out of the common law.

Statutory Redemption: The right of the defaulted property owner to recover the property after its sale by paying the appropriate fees and charged.

Step-Rate Mortgage: A mortgage that allows for the interest rate to increase according to a specified schedule (i.e., seven years), resulting in increased payments as well. At the end of the specified period, the rate and payments will remain constant for the remainder of the loan.

Stockholders' Equity: The sum of proceeds from the issuance of stock and retained earnings, less amounts paid to repurchase common shares.

Stripped MBS (SMBS): Securities created by "stripping" or separating the principal and interest payments from the underlying pool of mortgages into two classes of securities, with each receiving a different proportion of the principal and interest payments.

Sub-Prime Loan: "B" Loan or "B" paper with FICO scores from 620 - 659. "C" Loan or "C" Paper with FICO scores typically from 580 to 619. An industry term used to describe loans with less stringent lending and underwriting terms and conditions. Due to the higher risk, sub-prime loans charge higher interest rates and fees.

Subordinate: To place in a rank of lesser importance or to make one claim secondary to another.

Subdivision: A tract of land divided by the owner, known as the subdivider, into blocks, buildings lots, and streets according to a recorded subdivision plats, which must comply with local ordinances and regulations. A housing development that is created by dividing a tract of land into individual lots for sale or lease.

Subletting: The leasing of premises by a lessee to a third party for a part of the lessee's remaining term. See also "Assignment."

Subordinate Financing: Any mortgage or other lien that has a priority that is lower than that of the first mortgage.

Subordination: Relegation to a lesser position, usually in respect to a right security.

Subordination Agreement: A written agreement between holders of liens on a property that changes the priority of mortgage, judgment, and other liens under certain circumstances.

Subsidized Second Mortgage: An alternative financing option known as the Community Seconds® mortgage for low- and moderate-income households. An investor purchases first mortgage that has a subsidized second mortgage behind it. The second mortgage may be issued by a state, county, or local housing agency, foundation, or nonprofit corporation. Payment on the second mortgage is often deferred and carries a very low interest rate (or no interest rate). Part of the debt may be forgiven incrementally for each year the buyer remains in the home.

Substitution of Trustee: A written document that appoints a successor trustee to the trustee named in the deed of trust, (or present trustee). This document must be acknowledged by a notary public and recorded with the county recorder in the county in which the property is located.

Surety Bond: An agreement by an insurance or bonding company to be responsible for certain possible defaults, debts, or obligations contracted for by an insured party; in essence, a policy insuring one's personal and/or financial integrity. In the real estate business, a surety bond is generally used to ensure that a particular project will be completed at a certain date or that the contract will be performed as stated.

Survey: A property diagram that indicates legal boundaries, easements, encroachments, rights of way, improvement locations, etc. Surveys are conducted by licensed surveyors and are normally required by the lender in order to confirm that the property boundaries and features, such as buildings and easements, are correctly described in the legal description of the property.

Sweat Equity: Using labor to build or improve a property as part of the down payment.

TS138: See "Transmittal Form."

Tax Credit: An amount by which tax is owed is reduced directly.

Tax Deed: An instrument, similar to a certificate of sale, given to a purchaser at a tax sale. See also "Certificate of Sale."

Tax Lien: A charge against property, created by operation of law. Tax liens and assessments take priority over all liens.

Tax Sale: A court-ordered sale of real property to raise money to cover delinquent taxes.

Temporary Restraining Order (TRO): A judicial order, which is granted by a judge of the Superior Court. This order temporarily prohibits the trustee from proceeding with any further action under a specific foreclosure file until a trial is held or settlement reached. A TRO is effective, generally, for a 21-day time period or until a hearing is held and the judge decides whether a preliminary injunction will be granted or denied.

Tenancy by the Entirety: A form of joint tenancy held by husband and wife. Title automatically transfers to the survivor upon the death of one party. Neither party can sell or divide the property without the consent of the other. A type of joint tenancy of property that provides right of survivorship and is available only to a husband and wife. Contrast with tenancy in common.

Tenancy in Common: Title held by two or more people where each person can sell their interest without the consent of the other owners. There are no rights of survivorship. A type of joint tenancy in a property without right of survivorship. Contrast with tenancy by the entirety and with joint tenancy.

Tenant: One who holds or possesses lands or tenements by any kind of rights or title. A unit or activity of one military agency that receives services and occupies facilities provided by another military agency through a mutually developed written or oral agreement.

Terms: The period of time and the interest rate agreed upon by the lender and the borrower to repay a loan.

Time-Share: A form of ownership interest that may include an estate of interest in property and which allows use of the property for a fixed or variable time period.

Title: A legal document establishing the right of ownership and is recorded to make it part of the public record. Also known as a Deed.

Title 1: An FHA-insured loan that allows a borrower to make non-luxury improvements (like renovations or repairs) to their home; Title I loans less than $7,500 don't require a property lien.

Title Company: A company that specializes in examining and insuring titles to real estate.

Title Defect: An outstanding claim on a property that limits the ability to sell the property. Also referred to as a cloud on the title.

Title Insurance: Insurance that protects the lender against any claims that arise from arguments about ownership of the property; also available for homebuyers. An insurance policy guaranteeing the accuracy of a title search protecting against errors. Most lenders require the buyer to purchase title insurance protecting the lender against loss in the event of a title defect. This charge is included in the closing costs. A policy that protects the buyer from title defects is known as an owner's policy and requires an additional charge.

Title Search: A check of public records to be sure that the seller is the recognized owner of the real estate and that there are no unsettled liens or other claims against the property.

Toll: To temporarily stop. Frequently used to describe the tolling (stopping) during bankruptcy of any further acts in foreclosure.

Total Expense Ratio: Total obligations as a percentage of gross monthly income. The total expense ratio includes monthly housing expenses plus other monthly debts.

Transfer Agent: A bank or trust company charged with keeping a record of a company's stockholders and canceling and issuing certificates as shares are bought and sold.

Transfer of Ownership: Any means by which ownership of a property changes hands. These include purchase of a property, assumption of mortgage debt, exchange of possession of a property via a land sales contract or any other land trust device.

Transfer Taxes: State and local taxes charged for the transfer of real estate. Usually equal to a percentage of the sales price.

Transmittal Form (TS138): This is the "Request to Prepare Notice of Default" transmittal form, which is completed by the lender and forwarded to T.D. Service Company together with the note, deed of trust, assignments, and other necessary loan documents. This form sets forth all pertinent information to enable us to prepare the default documents.

Treasury Index: Can be used as the basis for adjustable rate mortgages (ARMs). It is based on the results of auctions that the U.S. Treasury holds for its Treasury bills and securities.

Truth-in-Lending: A federal law obligating a lender to give full written disclosure of all fees, terms, and conditions associated with the loan initial period and then adjusts to another rate that lasts for the term of the loan.

Trust: A fiduciary arrangement whereby property is conveyed to a person or institution, called a trustee, to be held and administered on behalf of another person, called a beneficiary. The one who conveys the trust is a trustor. Confidence placed in someone by giving him or her property to be held or used for another's benefit. The property held in trust.

Trustee's Deed Upon Sale: A written document, which is prepared and signed by the trustee when the secured property is sold at a trustee's sale. This document transfers ownership to the successful bidder at the sale; must be recorded with the county recorder in the county in which the property is located.

Trustee's Sale: The public auction of the real property, described in the deed of trust, to satisfy the unpaid obligation.

Trustee's Sale Guarantee: A title report given to the present trustee when a trustee's sale proceeding has been initiated. This report provides the names of the current owner, all liens and encumbrances recorded, and other information pertinent to the foreclosure process. The information is insured to be correct by the title company.

Trustee's Sale Proceeding (Foreclosure): The term used to describe the non-judicial procedure followed by the trustee in enforcing a creditor's rights when a debt secured on real property is in default.

Trustor: The borrower (or property owner) at the time the deed of trust was created. Trustor is often used to refer to the current owner.

Two Step Mortgage: An adjustable-rate mortgage (ARM) that has one interest rate for the first five to seven years of its term and a different interest rate for the remainder of the term.

Underwriting: The process of analyzing a loan application to determine the amount of risk involved in making the loan; it includes a review of the potential borrower's credit history and a judgment of the property value.

Unlawful Detainer Action (eviction): A legal action to remove someone who has unjustly retained possession of real property after one's right to possess has terminated.

Unsecured Loan: A loan that is not backed by collateral.

Up Front Charges: The fees charged to homeowners by the lender at the time of closing a mortgage loan. This includes points, broker's fees, insurance, and other charges.

Usury: Charging interest at a higher rate than the maximum rate established by state law.

VA (Department of Veterans Affairs): A federal agency, which guarantees loans made to veterans; similar to mortgage insurance, a loan guarantee protects lenders against loss that may result from a borrower default.

VA Mortgage: A mortgage guaranteed by the Department of Veterans Affairs (VA).

Valid: A condition that is legally sufficient; that will be upheld by the courts.

Variable Expenses: Costs or payments that may vary from month to month, for example, gasoline or food.

Variance: A special exemption of a zoning law to allow the property to be used in a manner different from an existing law.

Vendor: A seller, usually under the terms of a land contract.

Vested: A point in time when you may withdraw funds from an investment account, such as a retirement account, without penalty. However, taxes may be due on any funds that are actually withdrawn.

Void: Having no legal force or binding effect. Incurable.

Voidable: A condition capable of being made void, although not necessarily void in itself.

Voluntary Lien: A lien placed on property with the knowledge and consent of the property owner.

Walk Through: The final inspection of a property being sold by the buyer to confirm that any contingencies specified in the purchase agreement, such as repairs, have been completed, fixture and non-fixture property is in place, and confirm the electrical, mechanical, and plumbing systems are in working order.

Warranty Deed: A legal document that includes the guarantee the seller is the true owner of the property, has the right to sell the property and there are no claims against the property.

Will: A written document, properly witnessed, providing for the transfer of title to property owned by the deceased, called the testator.

Withdrawn Public Lands: Public domain lands held back for the use or benefit of an agency by reservation, withdrawal, or other restriction for a special government purpose. Withdrawn lands are typically used for national parks, wildlife refuges, and national defense. Withdrawal of public lands generally has the effect of segregating such land from lease, sale, settlement, or other disposition under the public land laws.

Wraparound Loan: A method of refinancing in which the new mortgage is placed in secondary, or subordinate, position; the new mortgage includes both the unpaid principal balance of the first mortgage and whatever additional sums are advanced by the lender. In essence, it is an additional mortgage in which another lender refinanced a borrower by lending an amount without disturbing the existence of the first mortgage.

Wraparound Mortgage: A mortgage that includes the remaining balance on an existing first mortgage, plus an additional amount requested by the mortgagor. Full payments on both mortgages are made to the wraparound mortgagee, who then forwards the payments on the first mortgage to the first mortgagee.

Zoning: Local laws established to control the uses of land within a particular area. Zoning laws are used to separate residential land from areas of non-residential use, such as industry or businesses. Zoning ordinances include many provisions governing such things as type of structure, setbacks, lot size, and uses of a building.

Zoning Ordinance: An exercise of police power by a municipality to regulate and control the character and use of property.

A free Comprehensive Glossary is available online at:
www.theloanmodguru.com

SECTION ELEVEN

SAVE YOUR HOME SUCCESS STORIES

SUCCESS STORIES

MEET WADET

Assume Nothing:
When NOT to believe everything you are told by the bank—you know what assuming does...

W adet is a single mother of three beautiful girls. When Wadet purchased her home during the housing boom, she was full of pride and joy for becoming a first time homebuyer. She didn't buy more than she could afford at the time. Wadet knew about being a wife and mother and working hard. She trusted the professionals to guide her through the loan process, as she didn't necessarily understand how it all worked and what type of loan she was getting. I know we all have to be responsible for our actions and for what we take on, but Wadet thought she understood the process and was convinced she was getting certain terms. She trusted the professionals to a fault.

Wadet was newly married, and her housekeeping business was going great. Along with the housing boom, came a surplus of work; a thriving economy meant people had extra money to spend on housekeeping. Wadet bought her home knowing she could afford it, and she even had a little nest egg saved up for an emergency.

What Wadet didn't know was that she would later become a victim of domestic abuse, followed by a downturn in the economy, a pending divorce, and no child support for her three children. Who knew that her clients would also lose their jobs, income, and homes? Who knew that she would not be able to count on her husband for financial support and that people would start cutting back and cleaning their own homes? Who knew that she would be unable to make her mortgage payment? This is exactly what happened.

Wadet immediately asked her parents to move in with her and help her pay the mortgage, but because she had an adjustable rate mortgage, the rate soon changed, and she found herself drowning in debt and not being able to make the higher payment.

Unfortunately, since many people are suffering through this crisis, there are unscrupulous people who prey on those who don't understand the system. They didn't understand it going into the loan, and they don't understand how to save their home, how to talk to their lender, what to say, or what to do. A realtor involved with her church advised Wadet that the ONLY thing she should and could do was to sell her modest town home through a short sale. Did the realtor ask her what she really wanted? NO, she told her that this was all that she could do. This kind of activity seems to go on a lot these days, and it is self-serving and wrong. Professionals need to do what is in the best interest of others and take into consideration their wishes, not their own greedy self-interests. But that's just me; who am I to judge the actions of others?

Since Wadet is not a real estate professional or well versed in complicated financial matters, she has experienced a lot of difficulties understanding everything involved. This is not difficult just for her, but to the average person trying to navigate this process, and she believed and trusted this realtor and allowed her and put her house up for sale. Never once did the realtor ask Wadet whether or not she wanted to try to fight for her home. Whose interest is being served here? The realtor even showed up with a moving van without consulting Wadet and told her she was moving her out because her house would show better and may sell faster with her out of it. Can you believe this?

Wadet never really wanted to lose her home or sell it, but she thought that was her ONLY option. Lucky for me, I met Wadet, and her beautiful heart and that of her parents and children have touched my life ever since. My life will never be the same, and neither will hers. When we sat down and talked, I learned that she did, indeed, want to keep her home. We began to compile her hardship letter, her income, her parents' income, and expenses. Her Trustee Sale was in two days, so we had to hurry. Postponing the sale was the #1 priority. I contacted the lender and advised them that we were going to fight to save the home and that we would be submitting an application for a loan modification. After more than five phone calls and several hours of work, we accomplished the task of postponing the sale. Now we could work the numbers correctly and piece together an organized package for the lender. We followed the protocol suggested by the lender and sent in the request. Once the package was submitted, we continued to contact the lender on a schedule of approximately two times per week and kept a close eye on the sale date to make sure no mistakes were made. We set up alerts and reminders to make sure the sale was postponed during the process that can usually take months to complete. I reassured Wadet, who was very nervous in the beginning of the process, but soon she realized I was on her side and what mattered to her mattered to me. I treated this case like I do all others, as if it was my own home. Soon Wadet no longer was under stress, because she saw that there was no doubt in my mind that we would get her loan modified. The process is not easy, and it does not happen overnight; but much like everything in life, nothing good comes easy. Everything good takes effort, faith, belief and determination, including loan modification.

I would love to say that the loan modification was approved the first time, but this was not the reality. You may be going through this right now, so you may know that this is the way it is. Unfortunately, most banks don't make the loan modification process easy. To their defense, most lenders were not prepared for the growing numbers of foreclosures and loan modifications that they would need to process internally. They have had to hire new people that may or may not know the guidelines themselves, and the employee workload has become too much to handle. This in turn builds internal stress on their part, not to mention emotional, scared, and many times angry homeowners calling all day.

No matter what they throw your way, negative or positive, you must remain calm, positive, and have an attitude of gratitude. Send your positive blessings to everyone you come into contact with, and if you don't get the answers you need from a particular person, call back or escalate to a supervisor, all the while keeping your inner peace and positive energy. Be prepared and have the right expectations because if you are prepared

SAVE YOUR HOME • SUCCESS STORIES

for it, somehow, it makes it just a little less frustrating. You are not alone in this.

I held my course, worked with Wadet to lower some expenses and find ways to increase her income. Once that was accomplished, we resubmitted her file. Unfortunately, we did not get the answers that we wanted. The numbers that her lender wanted to use were not the correct numbers, so we kept going and we fought it and fought it and kept track of our sale date. We got it postponed, and guess what? We got the modification. It was not quite what we needed, and the numbers were tight. Wadet could manage it, but we were exactly at the max payment she could make. She accepted the loan modification, as at that time, there were no government programs available.

I'd like to say she lived happily ever after, but unfortunately, and fortunately, this is not the end of the story. Six months into the new payment plan, the lender readjusted her impounds for her property taxes. They had promised to spread the back taxes over five years, and then all of a sudden, came back and did it over only 12 months. Her loan payment shot up to just as high as it was pre-modification.

I told Wadet that I would go back and work with her lender again to make sure they gave her an affordable payment, but Wadet was being influenced by people telling her to go see a loan modification attorney. The attorney was feeding Wadet promises of a possible loan cancellation or principal forgiveness, but he wanted to charge her thousands of dollars. In the end, he was still only going to process a regular loan modification and not the legal action she thought she was hiring him to take. When she found out that they were never going to litigate her case, she cancelled and came back to me. We went back to the lender and contacted the Home Preservation department, along with management, and accomplished our goals.

We were able to get Wadet a permanent modification from $2,982.57, that did not include her taxes and insurance, to $1,558.30, which included her taxes and insurance, along with other great term changes for her, plus adding her past due payments to the end of her loan and not having to bring all of this money in order to save her home. Mission accomplished. Wadet is very happy that this is something that is manageable for her and her family.

It is not easy to stay positive and determined when you are going through this process. It is certainly nerve wracking, especially if you are getting bad advice from people who don't always have your best interests at heart. Many times, they only confuse you more and emotions get in the way, with fear leading your every action. You MUST find a way to believe that you are going to get it done and then set out to make it happen, no matter what obstacle presents itself, including denials and unexpected changes that life throws your way. In Wadet's case, new programs became available by the time we had our final approval. Everything happens for a reason, and in this case, every event and time delay that occurred led to the final perfect outcome. Wadet and her family are still in their home, making the affordable payment that she obtained through her Home Affordable Modification Program approval.

It takes time for God's perfect plan to unfold. Keep the faith, expect ONLY Miracles, Question Authority, and don't give up.

MEET CONSTANTINE

Beware the Bait and Switch:
What to do when your bank offers you a modification that makes things worse, fight the good fight for what's right.

I n my opinion, Constantine is an unsung hero in America. I wish more people knew what an amazing contribution to society he makes on a daily basis as a special education teacher. He has incredible patience and a disposition about him that makes a difference to every person he meets. The world needs more people like Constantine, who go above and beyond to do the right thing for people.

Constantine suffered some economic hardships due to having to accept a lower paying job, something many people are doing in the current environment. This hardship resulted in Constantine not having enough income to make his mortgage payment, which jeopardized being able to save his longtime family home.

Constantine did not buy above his means, nor was he ever a subprime loan borrower. This housing crisis has been portrayed to be the fault of irresponsible homeowners, but for the most part, this portrayal is wrong. Hardships have fallen upon millions of people, companies, cities, states, and complete industries. Whoever can't see this must be hiding under a rock, as so many people have fallen victim to the crisis at hand. It can happen to anyone.

Last year, Constantine's request to Wells Fargo for the HAMP Home Affordable Modification Program was denied for failing the NPV Net Present Value Test. Unfortunately, his application was denied due to errors. It is not uncommon to fail this test, and it is not uncommon for errors to occur. When Constantine was declined for his loan modification request, he was offered an in house loan modification. The bad news is that it was not much different than what he was already paying, so it was not much help. Constantine felt there was a problem. He was not sure why he did not pass the NPV test. So many people are denied for this computer formula test, and most were never informed what the decline form letter even meant.

Denied for failed NPV is the extent of the explanation he received at that time. Now the denial notice has been expanded to include a little more information. This is the scenario; you have been waiting on pins and needles, you can barely sleep at night, and you can hardly perform your new job at half the pay for worry that you may also become homeless. NPV is all about profit. It tells the investor what is more profitable: helping the homeowner vs. foreclosure or short sale. When you fail NPV, to the homeowner, this means losing your home.

Most borrowers have no idea what an NPV calculator is and do not have a clue why they received a negative NPV test result. This prompted the Dodd-Frank Act, Section 1482, effective 02/01/2011, which attempts to resolve some of the confusion homeowners were faced with as a result of being denied due to a negative NPV test and the lack of an explanation. This act incorporates some accountability for servicers to provide much needed clarification of the information used to make the determination to homeowners so that they have access to check for accuracy of what is being used by the servicer.

Here is a typical notice most borrowers currently receive:

"...Negative NPV. The Home Affordable Modification Program requires a calculation of the net present value (NPV) of a modification using a formula developed by the Department of the Treasury. The NPV calculation requires us to input certain financial information about your income and your loan, including the factors listed below. When combined with other data in the Treasury model, these inputs estimate the cash flow the investor (owner) of your loan is likely to receive if the loan is modified and the investor's cash flow if the loan is not modified. Based on the NPV results, the owner of your loan has not approved a modification..."

During the HAMP waiting game, the weight of the pressure is overwhelming for most, and your mind starts racing to the worst-case scenario: "What if we lose our home?" And all you can get is a denial letter that feels like it is in another language, and the next letter tells you that you should sell your home. The problem is that Constantine, like so many others, was denied for HAMP in error. His income - teacher's pay - was inaccurately calculated, and he was almost forced to walk away from his home because of this mistake.

We contacted his servicer and requested the NPV values, the inputs that go into the NPV formula. At first, we were given the runaround, but after several letters and calls, we obtained the information. Then, we set forth to get the income and property value errors corrected, because we manually ran all of the numbers and came up with a reasonable calculation that gave clear indication that Constantine should have qualified for HAMP and should have passed the NPV test.

Constantine was told that if he escalated the errors, then the other in-house modification was off the table completely, so that if he failed HAMP, he would be given no other choices to save his home. This was a very unreasonable threat. Why would this be the case? Constantine should have the right to have the errors corrected and rerun HAMP without being pushed into accepting something else for fear of losing his home altogether. In Constantine's case, he had no choice but to forge on and go for it, because he could not afford the other payment. He advised his servicer that he wanted his file re-reviewed for HAMP, and it was yet again ran only for the in-house program.

When the inputs were received, we escalated his case to upper management. The first person again did not understand the reason for the request, so we escalated the case again, this time working with someone who understood exactly where the mistakes were and stayed with Constantine's case until the end. Constantine's correct numbers were finally used, and his corrected HAMP trial modification was approved and sent out. What a victory.

Five months later, when the permanent HAMP loan modification was sent out, it was back up to the incorrect payment, which was again a lot higher. Thank goodness the liaison representative we were working with was really great. When we advised him of this, he was able to go back to the negotiator in Loss Mitigation, get to the bottom of it, and correct it quickly, and the final correct loan modification arrived.

Constantine is ecstatic. He is so grateful to have saved his home for his family, and things are really starting to fall in place for him. He just got a new job closer to home with a great school district, and he is so happy to close this chapter of his life, taking from it the valuable lesson of determination and self advocacy, which begins with knowing your numbers, understanding the program, and taking focused action.

Scan with your smart phone to hear how Constantine saved his house NOW!"

Things can sometimes appear to be helpless, but there is hope. It is important to take a step back, take a deep breath and allow yourself to regroup. Getting out in nature and giving yourself some time to meditate can help you lower your stress level and provide you with an opportunity to gain the clarity you need to come up with an action plan, outside of the cloud of fear.

It is possible to appeal your findings. You are able to request the numbers that were used, and I highly believe you must do this and compare with your figures. If you find errors, you must put your appeal in writing immediately and challenge the errors. I cannot over stress the fact that you must know your financial numbers and how they fit in with the guidelines, as well as be prepared to be your own best advocate. Even if you go to an agency for help, if you don't know your information, how will you ever know if there are errors in what you are told or in a decision that can determine whether or not you save your home? Now is the time to be empowered.

Get informed, get empowered, and then Question Authority.

MEET MARIO AND BETTY

Not a Regular Paycheck:
How unconventional income may cost you your home if you don't present it correctly.

M ario has been a stuntman in Hollywood for a couple of decades, but none of the daring performances requiring his immense skill and danger could have adequately prepared him for what was to come from his request for loan modification assistance through the HAMP program.

Many people have felt that requesting a loan modification could be compared to jumping through fire rings, an acrobatic stunt, or even one of the greatest feats of your life, and for most homeowners, it is. Just as one would never attempt a stunt without preparation, one must never attempt a loan modification without training, courage, guts and ambition.

The movie industry, as many other industries, has taken a hit with the downward spiral of the economy, so for Mario, the stunt jobs were not coming as steadily as they had during previous times. His wife, Betty, was a real estate agent, an industry that was also hard hit. They wanted to concentrate on making a living and enlisted the help of a loan modification company, only to be deceived. They received no help from them, as well as several other attorney-based companies that disappeared with their money and left them hanging out to dry.

Betty then decided to become empowered with information to save their longtime home. We discovered that the reason her loan modification was declined was due to numerous errors made by the servicer of her loan. You see, Mario did not have a conventional paycheck. The movie studios pay for his stunt-work and royalties on an accumulating basis, which can be rather confusing for an underwriter. Since each studio provides a year to date paycheck, it makes it seem as though Mario makes more than he does.

Betty finally was finally able to get an approval for a HAMP loan modification, but the servicer, nevertheless, made a huge mistake in the payment calculation. They calculated the new payment just $50.00 less than what her normal payment was. Unfortunately, this was not only incorrect, but also, it would not have helped them save their home from foreclosure. This approval, as exciting as it seems when you are facing the loss of your home, was inaccurate. The servicer had used approximately $3,000 per month in excess income, causing an approximate $1,000 per month payment error. When the servicer was contacted, they said that it was the only HAMP approval they would get and they needed to take it or leave it, because they claimed it was correct and there was no way for them to change it under the HAMP rules.

I'm sorry, but this is a huge mistake, and I know for a fact that the HAMP program has no guideline stating that it cannot be reviewed when applications have been processed with errors in underwriting. Unfortunately, this is one type of incorrect answer that several thousand homeowners face. They are then railroaded into accepting inaccurate HAMP loan modifications for fear of losing their homes altogether, and because they cannot get someone to listen to them and correct errors, they are given a "take it or leave it" ultimatum. This is wrong. There is a systematic failure in the processing of this program, and it needs to be addressed from the top levels down. You are only as good as your weakest link. In corporate America, it is common for some of these systematic failures to fail to travel up the chain of command, although they should have a clue by now. I have seen lower level management cover up their service inconsistencies, first hand. It is up to us to get this information to the top of the corporate chain of command, if necessary, so that the breaks in this HAMP loan modification process can be fixed and changes can finally begin to be made.

Mario and Betty knew their accurate income and expense numbers thoroughly, and they knew that if the servicer followed the guidelines with these correct figures, they would qualify for the HAMP loan modification. They were confident that the right thing for them to do was fight on and make the servicer fix their mistakes. It was key for them to have their income methodically explained in an easy-to-understand manner to be able to show the underwriters at the servicer how Mario's income should be correctly calculated. When your income is not conventional, it is imperative that you know it and explain it, with a paper trail to back it up. Betty and Mario pressed on and escalated their case to several levels of their servicer's corporate offices until they were heard. After what seemed like something out of an action-packed suspense movie, Mario and Betty received their accurate HAMP loan modification approval, and they were able to save their home of many years.

Scan with your smart phone to hear how Betty saved her house NOW!"

Once you know your income and expense figures thoroughly and you know how they fit into the program guidelines, you can back up any escalation to management with confidence. Don't let an inaccurate denial or approval cost you your home. In every situation, you must become empowered with information to be your own best advocate.

To think for yourself, you must Question Authority.

MEET CARLA

Getting the Numbers Right:

How to overcome your fear and demand to be heard by your lender; they make mistakes—more mistakes than you think.

C arla is a social worker for Children's Services. She was making a decent income, while she did her part to help the children of her county. She did not buy a home above her means. The downturn in the economy caused furloughs in California and a loss of income for Carla, who now also had to care for an additional family member in her household and who also had unexpected health expenses.

Not many people are immune to the financial hardships that the state of the current economy has brought. Carla tried desperately to hang on as her savings dwindled to nothing. She had to dip into it just to stay afloat and try to maintain her then perfect credit rating. Now this, too, is gone.

It's July, 2009, and Carla was excited after several months of trying to get a HAMP loan modification that she was approved for a trial payment with Wells Fargo. One trial payment into the agreement, she received a phone call where she was told that they made a mistake in calculating her income, and now the payment was approximately $1,000 higher than the trial agreement specified. "Sorry," was all they could muster up in the empathy department.

Carla was devastated. There was no way she could afford this revised payment on her reduced income, and it was definitely not 31% of what her gross income was, as the HAMP program outlines in their guidelines. It turned out they were using her previous income in the new calculations vs. the new reduced income that caused the hardship. It would take over a full year to get someone to listen to the errors that were made and get the problem resolved.

In September of 2009, after the one trial payment was made and the next one was due with the new higher incorrect amount, Carla was able to finally get someone to listen to her story. This feat took dozens of phone calls, several emails, and overnight letters, but she finally got someone to listen rationally to the facts. Once again, she was happy to receive a revised and corrected trial payment, which came in December of 2009. Fast forward to June, 2010, after the trial payments that went on for more than the three specified for the program, when the permanent modification arrived...and lo and behold, it was back up to the incorrect amount. The new payment was approximately $1,000 over what the HAMP trial payment was, the same inaccurate calculation, the one that set this whole HAMP ordeal off in the first place. Can you imagine her dismay, her disappointment, and massive frustration? It took some coaxing to get Carla off of the proverbial HAMP ledge she had been perched on, now, for a full year.

The key here was in knowing what the correct payment was supposed to be, knowing that it still should qualify, and pushing and escalating this until someone would finally listen and fix the inaccuracies. Don't get me wrong; this can take some time, the road is long, and it will most definitely cause not a little, but a large amount of frustration. Still it is NOT impossible. I am not saying this is for the faint of heart, but I do believe in fighting for what is right, as long as you know what is right and are ready to back up your fight with accurate facts and go the distance.

I encouraged Carla that she could do this, to keep her faith and belief that she was fighting for her home and it was a worthy cause. There was no way she could keep her home if the error was not fixed. The values had dropped over 40% in her city; many of the neighborhoods had begun to look like ghost towns, reminiscent of the gold rush days in California. However, this was Carla's home, and she was determined to save her it.

Carla pressed on, this time taking it on as a challenge, the fight of her life to save her home from a needless foreclosure. There were numerous errors caused by the massive workload experienced during this foreclosure crisis, and it is evident that there is a clear breakdown within the HAMP processing factory at many of our nation's mortgage servicers. Carla is NOT the only person going through this sort of issue and so many other inaccuracies. Carla is one of thousands upon thousands of homeowners suffering through this painstaking process. Some people are lucky and have smooth sailing; many others are not quite so lucky.

The next battle for justice began immediately after reviewing the permanent HAMP modification and finding that the payment given was completely inaccurate, and it was not acceptable. Carla informed the processors of her HAMP permanent modification, only to be told that if she did not accept this, that she would not be able to reapply for HAMP. I think most people would have either accepted this inaccurate HAMP modification at this point, even if they could not afford it, or they would raise their white flag and give up. In fact, I am positive that this is something that happens on a daily basis because people are scared of losing their homes, and they also believe that their servicer, or their bank of many years would never intentionally steer them wrong or hurt them, so this must be their ONLY option; take it or leave it.

Carla chose to question authority, fight on, and fight hard. Carla fought with every ounce of her strength and with a sense of determination and belief that she would make it happen. Let me tell you, it was not an easy fight. This was a battle that was escalated at every level upon receiving the inaccurate HAMP loan modification in June of 2010, and this fight continued, upper level upon upper level, each department declining her request for the loan modification, now saying that Carla did not make enough to cover her debts. This was said, even when the inaccurate HAMP approval was inaccurate precisely because they had used an inflated income figure. This is why it is of utmost importance to know your numbers inside and out.

When you are empowered with the right information, you are able to push back at all levels with the confidence of knowing your stuff, in many cases, more than anyone else does. After Carla pushed back on the inaccurate HAMP modification, her loan was flagged, as if she did not accept the HAMP modification vs. the fact she just wanted an accurate approval.

Now every attempt at escalating her file, regardless of her explanation, was never re-run for the HAMP program. They kept running Carla's loan for other programs and turning her down based on other calculations, when all along Carla qualified for the HAMP loan modification, which is what she was trying to get them to see. She knew something was wrong because she had the figures in front of her and could see that there was no way she did not make enough to qualify for HAMP.

After several executive level escalations and hitting several walls, contact was made with Freddie Mac, her loan's investor. She was able to get someone to hear all the facts; they understood her initial request to fix the inaccuracies, and her file was re-run for HAMP.

I am proud to say that on December 20, 2010, and over one year and a half of going through the HAMP trials and HAMP tribulations, Carla got her Christmas miracle and was approved for an accurate HAMP permanent modification, and she is going to get to keep her home.

Get empowered; get knowledgeable about your situation and all of your options. Question Authority and Expect ONLY Miracles!

MEET HARRY

Eyes Wide Open: You must know your income better than the bank and know what you are applying for; to fight for your home, you need to be one step ahead.

Harry is a professional visual artist who has been in business for himself for many years and has owned his home for quite some time, as well.

Harry did not buy above his means. His area has a high cost of living, but Harry had a thriving business; in fact, he had even done freelance work for many big corporations when the economy was doing better and more money was in their budgets.

When the mortgage meltdown began, Harry did not even think it would affect him, but it really did. Little did he know that he was about to embark on one of the most difficult journeys of his life, the fight to save his family home.

As his customers began to cut back, Harry's income took a big hit. Harry was a very responsible family man and the thought of not being able to meet his obligation tore him up inside. The stress started to affect his concentration on developing new business, and his health even showed signs of deterioration, as he could not even sleep at night. Harry began to worry day and night about what to do about his bills and his mortgage. How would he ever get out of this downward spiral?

He decided to apply for HAMP. What he thought was going to be a helpful situation put him deeper and deeper in the hole and made him almost paralyzed in the fear of potentially losing his home. The anguish he felt was almost unbearable. He went to an agency for assistance, but yet again, he was denied, and no one really understood why.

The problem was in not understanding his income as a self-employed borrower and how the bank would view his application. In a time where businesses were cutting back, Harry also needed to revisit his company's budget and outgoing expenses. He tried again and reapplied on his own after that, and he was denied again.

Harry quickly realized in the words of Albert Einstein that "the definition of insanity is doing the same thing over and over again and expecting different results." Something had to change, or Harry would lose everything he has worked so hard for.

When desperate times call for desperate measures, the logical steps of lowering expenses and finding ways to increase profit are not always crystal clear. It is especially difficult to focus on taking the right action when your thoughts are frozen in anxiety and despair. It took a while for Harry to get himself back on track and regroup, but once he had clear goals and targets he needed to reach, he was able to execute his plan and strive for the changes he had to make in his business model to save his home.

Next, he realized he did not understand the program he was applying for, so he began to empower himself with information so he would know exactly where he stood before he sent in his modification package to Bank of

America, this fourth, and hopefully final, time. He began to meditate, get closer to God, and think and act positive, determined, focused and with a real knowing that he would succeed and would not give up until he saved his home.

Unfortunately, his resubmission initially met with resistance, and he could not get anyone to see the months and months of work Harry had done in his business as they kept reverting to the numbers he had submitted in late 2009, versus taking into account the great changes Harry had strived so hard to make in 2010. He had to put together some escalation letters, be persistent in his endeavor to succeed, and not take no for an answer.

Harry finally got someone to listen to his case, and his new application was finally accurately reviewed. Less than one month later, Harry was approved for his affordable and permanent loan modification.

Now Harry and his family can smile for the camera and say HAMP! Harry saved his home, and he also learned some valuable lessons in perseverance, resilience, and self-advocacy, not to mention the power of positive thinking to improve all aspects of your life.

Scan with your smart phone to hear how Harry saved his house NOW!"

"Whatever the mind of man can conceive and believe, it can achieve."

- Napoleon Hill

SECTION TWELVE

RELATED LINKS AND CLOSING INFORMATION

COMMENTARY

DAVID M. CORBIN

A s an author and speaker, I love people like Anna Cuevas who are truly passionate about what they do. *Save Your Home* conveys the passion that Anna has to help people and motivate them to take all the steps necessary to protect their property and their rights, especially during trying times.

In this book, Anna emphasizes the same concept developed in my book, *Illuminate*, which states that a problem not addressed never goes away. In fact, it usually gets bigger. That's precisely why Anna stresses that the time to act to save your home is now. Face that you have a problem, find out what the problem is, and then get to work immediately to fix it.

I've known Anna for years and am increasingly impressed with her fortitude as she strives to help thousands of deserving homeowners protect their assets and turn their circumstances around. What impresses me the most, though, is that she portrays and encourages an incredibly positive attitude, especially during stressful times. Because of this, Anna could be the poster woman for my book, which states that the key to facing, finding, and fixing negative situations is to deal with them in a strictly positive light. Shed light on the problem, take her advice and follow her proven system to fix it, and keep a calm, positive, and healthy attitude. When you do, you'll be better able to state your facts, provide viable solutions, and save your home.

In this book, you have everything you need to save your home—including Anna's wealth of knowledge and experience and her inspiration, motivation, and faith. Add to that her encouragement and unrelenting commitment to her cause, and you can see that while *Save Your Home* is the most comprehensive resource for at-risk homeowners everywhere, Anna Cuevas is their biggest supporter and advocate.

You didn't ask for your problem, but you can fix it. Follow Anna Cuevas' step-by-step process to do just that. Now, get to work. Illuminate the negative, turn it into a positive, and save your home.

David M. Corbin

Speaker and Author of *Illuminate*

ENTREPRENEURS CREED

I do not choose to be a common man,
It is my right to be uncommon...if I can,
I seek opportunity....not security.
I do not wish to be a kept citizen,
Humbled and dulled by having the state looking after
me.
I want to take the calculated risk;
To dream and to build,
To fail and to succeed.
I refuse to barter incentive for a dole;
I prefer the challenges of life
To the guaranteed existence;
The thrill of fulfillment
To the state of calm Utopia.
I will not trade freedom for beneficence
Nor my dignity for a handout.
I will never cower before any master
Nor bend to any threat.
It is my heritage to stand erect,
Proud and unafraid;
To think and act for myself,
To enjoy the benefit of my creations
And to face the world boldly and say:
This, with God's help, I have done.
All this is what it meant
To be an Entrepreneur.

(Excerpt from *Common Sense*, written in 1776, by
Thomas Paine)

IN CLOSING

I am very proud of your determination to Save Your Home. Although there are no guarantees in this life, absolutely nothing will happen if we do not take our destiny into our own hands and take action. My wish for you is that this book gives you the insight and knowledge you need to fight back and save your home. That being said, please don't lose sight of the fact that your health and family are more important than anything material could ever be, and in the big scheme of things, the important things should always come first.

I wish you much success in fighting to Save Your Home. You are always in my prayers.

"You don't have to be great to get started, but you have to get started to be great." ~ Les Brown

Your friend,

Anna Cuevas–Expect Only Miracles and Question Authority

PS: I would love to hear your success stories and see a picture of your family – perhaps your story can inspire others to forge on and pay it forward. We could all be ripples of hope in this vast ocean of possibility.

success@askaloanmodguru.com

ABOUT ANNA CUEVAS

How Does an Award Winning Ex-Bank Executive Turn into America's Loan Modification Guru?

If there was a superhero in the loan modification industry, Anna Cuevas would be it...cape and all. Proudly helping thousands of people save their homes and overturning countless foreclosures, Anna is a power-punched, fiery woman with a "take no prisoners" mentality. Her temerity in surviving ovarian cancer is just one more stripe that has fueled her into becoming an advocate for homeowners nationwide.

America's Loan Modification Guru

She has become the symbol for empowerment and a guardian to thousands of fearful homeowners that are faced with the hardship and stigma of losing their home. Providing a powerful resource and toolbox to guide homeowners in the right direction, she: offers proven step-by-step solutions, has taken the guesswork out of the application process, deciphered the legal jargon, and unveiled insider secrets. With Anna on their side, homeowners can now replace stress and agony with viable ways to fight back.

A Trusted Advocate for Advocates

Noting the overwhelmingly misguided information blanketing the media, Anna is no stranger to the countless stories of homeowners being advised that foreclosure is their sole option. She lights up knowing that most are not even aware of their rights and are inaccurately declined by banks.

Anna equips people with the educational fortitude to climb out of the victim trap, and in doing so, has become a trusted advocate for advocates. Her brazen approach teaches homeowners to be one step ahead of the banks, defend their homes, and stop foreclosure. With consumer strategy training, she endorses homeowners to be their own best advocate. She has held the hand of the everyday man, from attorneys, single moms, police, to ice cream truck owners. Her gift in helping others has garnered rave reviews echoing the same words over and over again: "Thank you so much. I didn't know I could fight back."

You Don't Become a #1 Lender in the U.S. if You Don't Know What You Are Doing

With over 25 years in Real Estate and Banking working for a Fortune 500 lender, Anna has extensive knowledge in home loans and the refinancing industry. She was ranked #1 Business Development Sales Producer in the U.S., Top 1% Sales Performer (President's Club) four years in a row, and holds the all-time record for loan production. It's no surprise that Anna was recently nominated for CNN Heroes.

She is a number one bestselling author of *Fight for Your Dreams*, with Les Brown, a featured blogger for *The Huffington Post,* contributor for *Ezine* and *Articlesbase,* founder of *Ask a Loan Mod Guru*, featured in *FUSEing Families Magazine*, and is seen on the online Web TV show *Main Street Marketing Machine.*, and is launching a "Save Your Home" grassroots movement dedicated to empowering homeowners across America.

Her slogan, "Expect only miracles and question authority," has become a mantra for thousands coast to coast. She has personally answered over 3,000 blog posts from suffering homeowners seeking guidance and helping to reverse the powerlessness behind foreclosure. Caped and soaring high, Anna's mission is to transform homeowners into proud crusaders with the knowledge and strength to become their own superhero.

As a labor of love, Anna created askaloanmodguru. Thousands of people visit this resource site and blog to gain knowledge, inspiration, and hope.

It is her hope that you, too, are inspired in your journey to save your home.

She can't wait to hear your success story!!

To learn more or to visit Anna's blog, please visit:
www.theloanmodguru.com

Articles by Anna Cuevas are available at:
www.huffingtonpost.com/anna-cuevas

Join our community on Facebook:
www.facebook.com/loanmodguru

Comprehensive Do It Yourself System
Available at
www.theloanmodguru.com

INCLUDES:

- An easy to use step-by-step loan modification application software which populates into Making Home Affordable RMA forms

- Video step by step directions guiding your every step

- Your calculated debt ratio, or DTI, both before the proposed loan modification, as well as after the proposed modification request

- User friendly budget populated into the detailed monthly expense worksheet

- User friendly detailed monthly income worksheet

- Lender ready checklist takes the guesswork out of what to submit

- A personalized hardship letter template that allows you to fill in the blanks and customize it to fit your situation

- A bank ready proposal asking for a specific result

- A HAMP program calculator built in to see how your financial picture fits into the current HAMP modification terms

- The calculator shows you how much forbearance would be necessary so you know before you apply how the bank will see this figure
- An NPV calculator
- A Profit and Loss form template for self-employed borrowers
- Fax coversheet
- Loan modification request letter
- Online blog support if you are stuck

Get yours at www.TheLoanModGuru.com

To order more copies of this book & inquire about volume discounts,

please contact us directly at:

sales@volitionpress.com

"Ask, and it shall be given you; seek; and you shall find; knock and it shall be opened unto you. For every one that asketh receiveth; and he that seeketh findeth; and to him that knocketh it shall be opened."

REMARKS POSTED AT THELOANMODGURU.COM

Hi Anna,
You site is a Godsend. I wish I knew of it earlier. Thank you for everything you are doing to help everyone and to keep your readers positive and hopeful. Helping people save their homes is such an important and vital need in this economy. So many don't know where to turn and are unable to get proper assistance. ~ Vickie

Anna, thank you so much for sharing your knowledge and inspiring all of us that are struggling and fighting for our home. In this battlefield, we need as much camaraderie as possible to prevail. I have been struggling since Sept. 2010 and still fighting. We won't take NO as an answer, we can't. Pretty soon I may need your help, but meanwhile, may God bless you for all the help that you are providing to all of us. ~ Carrie H

Thanks so much for what you do! ~ Jane

Hello Anna. Your website is amazing. I am learning so much. ~ Cindy C.

Hi Anna! I have searched for answers site after site. I am grateful for your site. ~ Dwynne

Hi. Thank you for having this hopeful site. ~ Karen K

Hi Anna,
I am so glad I found this site. Thank you in advance for your help. ~ Jamilla

Hello Anna, your website is great. ~ Tina A

Hi Anna,
Thanks for the valuable information that you provide. ~Michelle

Hi Anna,
I have been out of touch for awhile but I came across your site today. I wanted to thank you so much for helping me out years ago. I will be eternally grateful to you for that. This was back in 2008. You are the best! Thank you again! many blessings to you Anna. ~Cindy H.

You rock Anna! Blessings and have a wonderful weekend. We appreciate all that you do. :) ~Joseph

More people need to know that help is available and they don't have to roll over and lose their homes. ~Beryl

Hi Anna,
I want to thank you from bottom of my heart for all the useful information and specially the quote "Expect Miracles" my mod application was denied for negative NPV from the bank and set for FCL. After reading info on ur site. I submitted my dispute to Office of president. Got a call from that office and was told that all FCL has been suspended and my file is under review by Executive office and assured me that they will resolve it in a matter which is suitable for me. Thanks again and keep up the Noble work u doing. ~ Sincerely, Z

Words cannot describe what Anna Cuevas did for me and my situation! I like many good Americans was a casualty of the recession which hit the good ole USA in 2008. I was a mortgage loan officer for a bank who always paid his bills on time. Then when the roof caved in and I did not get a paycheck for 6 months even though I was still working. All of the mortgages that I was working on collapsed as all of my customers were feeling the results of our economy! All of my hard work went down the tubes and their was no compensation and my situation just spiraled downward! I contacted my lender relentlessly trying to modify my mortgage! There was plenty of grandstanding by the government stating that everyone would be taken care of, but I can't tell you the roadblocks I ran into! I was confident with my expertise in the mortgage industry that I could rectify my situation and lord knows I gave it everything I had, but I was swimming up stream and going under fast with foreclosure breathing down my neck. I had a good feeling about Anna and her claims that she could help me!

Anna Cuevas was better than advertised! She was genuine, knowledgeable and willing to listen and advise me on my situation with confidence and concern which was very much welcome after getting my fanny kicked for two years. After pulling the trigger and putting my fate in her hands the results were astounding and quick!. Her format and contact information for my lender was dead on! I got a response in no time and before you knew it I was offered a loan modification! The cost for this service was well worth it and to be honest I would have paid double! My gut told me that Anna was different! Her sincerity was unique and genuine and when she says she enjoys helping people this is from her heart and I can tell you first hand that there is no hidden agenda here! If you need help then stop worrying and pull the trigger and thank your lucky stars that you have found Anna Cuevas. Good luck! ~Jim N. Red Bank, NJ

WHAT OTHER EXPERTS ARE SAYING ABOUT *SAVE YOUR HOME* AND ANNA CUEVAS

Anna Cuevas champions the characteristics I encourage all entrepreneurs to follow. In Save Your Home, she answers the most frequently asked questions, while telling them everything they should know to succeed at keeping their home. In this book, she has created one of the most valuable resources for at-risk homeowners everywhere.
~Mike Koenigs, Traffic Geyser

Save Your Home is the most important book to understanding the loan modification process. It gives the reader hope and the right knowledge to move through the process forearmed and forewarned! A must for these times!
~Jill Lublin, jilllublin.com International speaker and bestselling author of 3 books, including *Get Noticed...Get Referrals* (McGraw Hill)

In these times of financial crisis, Save Your Home is an absolute must read for struggling homeowners who are desperately trying to hang on to their houses. Anna Cuevas, America's foremost loan modification expert, empowers readers in this easy to understand, step-by-step handbook on how to effectively deal with creditors and save your home. Beyond the educational value contained in this book, you will also read her passion and

willingness to help thousands of people remain homeowners. Definitely a must read.
~Elizabeth Karwowski, Get Credit Healthy, Inc.

This is the "go to" book for loan modification. Anna brings 26 years of experience in the mortgage industry, coupled with her unmatched work on behalf of her clients faced with foreclosure, and has put it all together in this comprehensive guide to loan modification. I have witnessed Anna as a true student of how to get results. This book is a must read for anyone looking into a loan modification.
~Mark D. Potter, Attorney, POTTER HANDY, LLP

CREDITS:

BOOK ANGEL/EDITOR: Jane Komarov

LAYOUT/EDITOR: Patti McKenna

COVER DESIGN: Wesley Bryant, www.worldvoice.com

DESIGN CONCEPTS: Karen Barranco, www.SpecialModernDesign.com

COVER IMAGE: Getty Images

BIO: Lisa Cafiero; Write the First Time

BOOK ART DRAWINGS: Jeannel King, Process Arts and Facilitation

OTHER BOOKS BY ANNA CUEVAS

Available today at:

www.TheLoanModGuru.com

CPSIA information can be obtained at www.ICGtesting.com
Printed in the USA
LVOW090643170512

282126LV00003B/272/P